LEADERSHIP

Compiled and edited by

William Safire

AND

Leonard Safir

SIMON AND SCHUSTER

New York · London · Toronto · Sydney · Tokyo · Singapore

SIMON AND SCHUSTER
Simon & Schuster Building
Rockefeller Center
1230 Avenue of the Americas
New York, New York 10020

Designed by Irving Perkins Associates
Manufactured in the United States of America

1 3 5 7 9 10 8 6 4 2

Library of Congress Cataloging in Publication Data

Leadership / [edited by] William Safire and Leonard Safir.
p.   cm.
1. Leadership—Quotations, maxims, etc.   I. Safire, William.
1929–   .   II. Safir, Leonard.
PN6084.L15L4   1990
082—dc20   89-29598
                                  CIP

ISBN 0-671-67536-2

To
David Mahoney,
who lives by this advice:
Never play not to lose;
Always play to win.

Contents

A
Preface
Quotation

When will men stop their questionings and recognize a leader when he rises? When will they gather to his standard and say, "We no longer question; we believe you; lead on, for we are behind you."

America needs men of that sort. Will you encourage them? Will you make your universities such places as can produce them?

. . . You are your own saviours, and when you have come to the determination to save yourselves you will know your leader the moment you meet him, for you will know if he is of your sort and of your purpose.

> —Woodrow Wilson
> Speech before the Princeton Club in
> Chicago, 1910

Prolegomenon

BY WILLIAM SAFIRE

The first rule of being a leader is to *focus on the challenge at hand*. That's because "being" a leader is secondary; before that state of being comes the act of leading. First comes the verb, *lead;* then follows the noun, *leadership*.

Nobody who will ever have a substantial following sits around thinking "What do I need to become a leader? How should I look, speak, handle myself before a crowd? What agents and advisers do I hire, what books and cassettes do I buy to grant me instant charisma and anoint me with command presence?"

On the contrary, potential leaders stare at the wall and plot: "Where do I want to take this company (or group, or army, or city, or nation)? How do I carry out my plan for getting from here-now to there-then?" Only with that plan, goal, or big idea firmly in mind does the leader-to-be turn to the nitty-gritty of ways to agitate others to vibrate on the same frequency. Only by doing the leading does the one positioned in front become a leader.

Don't confuse getting *in* front with getting *out* front. That's the difference between a principal and a spokesman, between a mover and a shaker. (Does the tone of this prolegomenon strike you as imperious and didactic? Excuse me, I'm leading.)

To repeat the first rule: *Focus on the challenge at hand*. That challenge might be a crisis, a chronic problem, or a sense of drift, to be met by your solution, your dream, or the whole new world inside your head. Set aside for the moment distractions like the

13

tricks of the leadership trade or the secrets of charismatic success; time for them later.

Charlie Grimm, manager of the Chicago Cubs in the thirties and forties, heard an excited report on a potential recruit from one of his scouts. "Charlie, I've landed the greatest young pitcher in the land," said the breathless scout. "He struck out every man who came to bat. Twenty-seven in a row. Nobody even got a foul until two were out in the ninth. The pitcher is right here with me. What shall I do?" Said the purposeful (although rarely successful) Charlie: "Sign up the guy who got the foul. We're looking for hitters."

That's focus—first things first. The primary purpose of the quotations herein, culled mainly by Len Safir (he's my brother, but I added an "e" to our family name as an aid to pronunciation), is to provide the putative leader with good advice about a sense of mission. That above all; then we make available the best ancient and modern advice about the secrets, methods, rules, and devices that make leading easier or more effective.

The key word is "advice." Do not search here for syrupy observation, or even the profound rumination that can be found in other anthologies. What we most often present here is hard, useful, practical advice about how to clamber up the greasy pole of success. Look for the verb in each of these apothegms, the direct bit of action called for in every adage. We slip in an observation or insight now and then when we can't help it, but the sharp edge of this book is its imperative counsel. (Here's some: be careful how you spell "apothegms," or better yet, throw out that unfamiliar word and substitute "truths." But wait: if short, familiar words are better than mouth-fillers, how come I call this foreword a "prolegomenon," which is synonymous with "preface" but has a scholarly connotation? To catch the eye, that's why; one trick of leadership is to attract the attention of potential followers.)

In this compilation, clear direction is all: President George Bush may say "You can't lead without knowing what you're talking about," but the reason we include that statement is that it is preceded by his finger-in-the-chest advice, "Do your homework." We have waded through reams of exemplary prose about the deleterious effect of task forces on productivity in business and politics, but what's in here is the boiled-down prudence of William Graham Sumner: "If you ever live in a country run by a committee, be on the committee."

In the leadership quotation dodge, it's vital to get ahead of the power curve. A leader, in our book, is first a purposeful pilot or guide; next a commander, boss, or chief; finally, and least important, a somebody, notable, or luminary. Here are further rules for the leadership artist, advice on traits to cultivate after the Grimm focus is achieved:

2. *Cultivate an air of detached involvement.* Isn't "detached involvement" an oxymoron, a jarring juxtaposition of opposites? Yes; the art of leadership demands subtlety and involves complexities. If it were simple, we'd call this book "The Business of Leadership" or, to appeal to the widest audience, "The Leadership Racket." We reject that approach; leadership is an art.

On the social level, "detached involvement" means getting close without getting cozy: "The commander must try, above all," wrote Field Marshal Erwin Rommel, "to establish personal and comradely contact with his men, but without giving away an inch of his authority." In politics, "detached involvement" means being of the people but not in the people's lap: "There can be no power without mystery," said Charles de Gaulle. "There must always be a 'something' which others cannot altogether fathom, which puzzles them, stirs them, and rivets their attention." In business, be a "hands-on" manager as much as you like, but keep one hand in your own pocket: "Never reveal all of yourself to other people," writes Michael Korda. "Hold back something in reserve so that people are never quite sure if they really know you." When following this rule, be careful not to overlook the next:

3. *Never lose the common touch.* "Remember the difference between a boss and a leader," says an engine foreman quoted herein. "A boss says 'Go!'—a leader says 'Let's go!' " Too obvious and corny? Perhaps; but in this particular rule, cornball may be played.

A strong and exciting tie exists between leader and those willingly led—of common interests, of shared values, of mutual affection. Shakespeare's proud General Coriolanus failed to win the support of the Romans because he failed to appreciate the requirements of the crowd. When he demanded to know the price of a man's vote for the consulship, Coriolanus was dumbfounded when told: "The price is, to ask it kindly." Two millennia later, Louisiana governor Huey Long was advising young politicians: "If you want some ham, you gotta go into the smokehouse."

4. *Hone your authenticity.* Being an authentic is hard. In an age that celebrates compromise and deems concession the better part of valor, the pressure is on to hold up a finger to the prevailing breeze and acquiesce. Too many would-be leaders smooth out their rough edges and round out their sharp corners until they resemble all the other pebbles in the stream. This kind of aimless amiability works only in organizations and societies that encourage their leaders to float to the top. "To get along, go along," advised Speaker Sam Rayburn, setting forth the non–battle cry of back-scratching politics; we are laden with strictures to use honey to attract flies, and with honing straps to sharpen communications skills.

But "beware of charisma," warns Daniel Boorstin, the historian. He calls that quality great leaders have in common "the need to be authentic. . . . While the charismatic has an uncanny outside source of strength, the authentic is strong because he is what he seems to be."

Twentieth-century leaders from Lenin and Churchill to Henry Ford and Lee Iacocca, from Albert Einstein and Andrei Sakharov to Margaret Thatcher and Ronald Reagan, are examples of authentics—people who generated great controversy and took a delight in cultivating mighty adversaries. The authentics in every field, the grand successes and the great flops, are remembered not for what they conceded but for what they refused to concede. They were followed or furiously abandoned because their principles were not fluid. They knew how to create the movement in a movement by refusing to budge.

The most authentic leader I have met was the Kurdish chieftain Mustapha al-Barzani. He was a little guy in an ill-fitting Western suit who spoke no English; his cause was ignored and his people reviled, but General Barzani had a presence, a carriage, an internal certainty, and a fierce look in his eyes that made the most skeptical visitor envision him in flowing robes leaping on a horse and seizing command of an unstoppable army. The slogan of his nationalist movement was *Pesh Merga*, which translates as this ultra-authentic's advice to "Go forward, forward—even unto death."

5. *Impress posterity by observing your posterior.* This is a euphemism for the punchy vulgarism "Watch your ass." (Do not confuse this sensible caution with CYA, "cover your ass," the papering-over of responsibility in group decision-making that is the

first refuge of a bad bureaucrat.) Every leader is vulnerable; he cannot properly face forward without exposing his back. If he does not check out his line of retreat, he invites trouble that could turn a retreat into a rout. (The male pronoun embraces the female, a simple, nonsexist rule that should be followed by all humankind.)

In that cautious respect, "Policy-making is not as easy as slurping down cabbage soup," Yegor Ligachev told a Soviet party congress rubber-stamping the policy of Mikhail Gorbachev. "Caution should be combined with decisiveness. As the saying goes, before going into the room, make sure you can get out again."

6. *To generate loyalty, deserve loyalty; to deserve loyalty, be loyal.* A curious adage is known to politicians: "If you don't go to other people's funerals, they won't come to yours." This calls up the vision of a funeral attended mainly by ghosts, but the meaning is clear: loyalty is a two-way street, and a narrow one to boot. Mutual loyalty includes fidelity (h'ray!) and patronage (boo!), toleration of shortcomings in recognition of past service, a pride in institutional continuity even in an era of portable pensions and merger mania. Rarely do we look to our leaders for justice; more often, we look for help. If they come through for us on the little things, we trust them on the big things, and our trust in them is the coin of their command of us.

"Do not betray a confidence and do not knife a comrade," wrote Stanley Walker, city editor of the New York *Herald Tribune* in the thirties. His dual commandments of loyalty and solidarity in journalism had a practical rationale: "The man who violates a confidence will lose his sources of news; the man who double-crosses a colleague will, on some bloody tomorrow, find himself naked and helpless."

7. *Take charge by giving clear, clean, understandable orders.*

Taking charge does not mean barking commands in all directions. It does not mean announcing your assumption of power, as Secretary of State Al Haig learned to his regret ("I'm in charge here").

Details count; the way you enter a room contributes to your command presence. I was a volunteer speechwriter for Richard Nixon in the sixties, when he was a walking political obituary; accompanying him on the way to a meeting, I pulled open the door and motioned him ahead into a crowded room. He shook his head. "Open the door wide, go in and clear the way," he ordered. I did what he asked. As the crowd inside quieted and focused its attention on the doorway, Nixon swept in briskly, all smiles and waves. The "studied entrance" makes a big impression.

Admirals are very good on orders, both taking and giving. Franklin Roosevelt told Frank Knox, his Secretary of the Navy, a few days after the attack on Pearl Harbor: "Tell Nimitz to get the hell to Pearl and stay there until the war is over."

That was clear enough, but what about unavoidable moments of ambiguity? Any eventuality can be handled with crispness. When Admiral William "Bull" Halsey received word of the Japanese surrender, he sent this message to the Third Fleet: "Cease firing, but if any enemy planes appear, shoot them down in a friendly fashion."

8. *Figure out what awaits you on the other side of the hill.* Military officers call it "intelligence," the product of "G-2"; business executives call it "market research," which makes possible "strategic planning"; street-smart politicians call it "a good sniffer." In every field, the prudent leader first explores the lay of the land.

"First see the hare, then loose the falcon," goes the Chinese proverb. (Another Chinese adage, conscious of the need for cost control in intelligence-gathering, warns: "Don't climb a tree to look for fish.") Mortimer Zuckerman, owner of *U.S. News & World Report,* puts it this way: "Before you build a better mousetrap, it helps to know if there are any mice out there."

Most people make the mistake of planning only on the basis of what they know. The trick is to lay what you do know against all there is to know, make the subtraction, and then try to find out as much as possible of the needed-to-know unknown. In writing a newspaper column, a pundit is tempted to parade his facts toward a triumphant conclusion, but the essays that work best are the result of putting frustration to work, looking at the gaps in the jigsaw puzzle, asking "What is happening that is not in the news— what's missing from the stories before us?"

"All the business of war," wrote the Duke of Wellington, "and indeed all the business of life, is to endeavor to find out what you don't know by what you do." The conqueror of Napoleon added: "That's what I called 'guessing what was on the other side of the hill.' "

9. *Discipline your thinking by forcing your thoughts to march on paper.* A ghostwriter is a crutch; when you see "as told to" on a book, recognize that the pseudo-author is too lazy, too shallow,

or too fearful of exposing confusion to write it himself. The leader who relies too heavily on others to write his most important words is one who will rely on staff to think his thoughts and set up his decisions.

Let me not foul an old nest: as a longtime White House ghost, I know that no President has time for churning out hundreds of messages to Congress and reams of incidental remarks known fondly as "Rose Garden rubbish." Time-saving assistance in framing a response or directive can hardly be faulted, as illustrated by Eisenhower's request to chief of staff Walter Bedell Smith: "Bedell, tell them to go to hell, but put it so they won't be offended." But writing is not merely a technique that a leader can purchase, like some sort of early version of the Teleprompter.

Writing is a means of thinking, of marshaling and refining ideas, and the leader who cannot write intelligently probably cannot think straight. Beautiful metaphors, nice turns of phrase, memorable slogans can be added to a leader's message, and ghostwriters and options-drafters come in handy to enliven prose and stretch the mind—but beware the commander who farms out all his writing, because he is a front for somebody else's thinking. Decisions should be arrived at, not "made"; speeches should be hammered out, worked through to combine policy and persuasive argument, not merely "delivered."

Not all leaders agree on this. ("Damn your writing, mind your fighting," muttered General Sir Archibald Wavell.) But Winston Churchill called himself "a strong believer in transacting official business by The Written Word." Body language, quick Q-and-A sound bites, smooth assurances and ad-lib rambles, oleaginous smears of platitudes and pieties—all these are the commercial greeting cards of business and political life, substitutes for genuine sentiment and on-the-record originality. The Written Word, as Churchill pointedly capitalized the phrase, is the product of a leader who is not fooling around. Don't treat writing as a knack unless you are prepared to think of thinking as a casual talent.

10. *Temper your vengeance; power can stay in shape without exercise.*

Amateurs in leadership like to flex their new muscles, dazzling themselves and their coteries with the play of power. They worry that if mastery is not frequently demonstrated, it may atrophy. "Use it or lose it" is their nervous motto. Old pros understand that power gains moral meaning in its restraint, and recall those who learned "abuse it and lose it." They are focused on the challenge at hand; they know when they are looking for hitters, and for hitters who know when to hit and when to refrain from swinging.

Robert E. Lee wrote that "the forbearing use of power . . . the power which the strong have over the weak" was the "test of a true gentleman." (Were he writing today, he would probably change "gentleman" to "person of honor and civility" because the human quality he was concerned with has nothing to do with a person's sex; in this sense, a woman is a "true gentleman.") In the following passage, which appears in this anthology under the important category of Character, the commander who was chosen to lead the Union armies, but who chose instead to lead the South in civil war, set down the advice that best exemplifies the art of leadership:

"The forbearing and inoffensive use of all this power or authority," wrote General Lee long after his surrender to a suddenly gentle General Grant at Appomattox, "or a total abstinence from it, when the case admits it, will show the gentleman in a plain light. The gentleman does not needlessly and unnecessarily remind an offender of a wrong . . . he strives for that nobleness of self and mildness of character which imparts sufficient strength to let the past be but the past."

A

ABC's of Leadership

Trust your subordinates. You can't expect them to go all out for you if they think you don't believe in them.

Develop a vision. . . . People want to follow someone who knows where he or she is going.

Keep your cool. The best leaders show their mettle under fire.

Encourage risk. Nothing demoralizes the troops like knowing that the slightest failure could jeopardize their entire career.

Be an expert. From boardroom to mail room, everyone had better understand that you know what you're talking about.

Invite dissent. Your people aren't giving you their best . . . if they are afraid to speak up.

Simplify. You need to see the big picture in order to set a course, communicate it, and maintain it.

> —From an article in *Fortune* by Kenneth Labich

Now there are five matters to which a general must pay strict heed. The first of these is administration; the second, preparedness; the third, determination; the fourth, prudence; and the fifth, economy.

> —Wu Ch'i (430–381 B.C.)

Four rules of leadership in a free legislative body:
First, no matter how hard-fought the issue, never get personal.
   Don't say or do anything that may come back to haunt you on
   another issue, another day. . . .
Second, do your homework. You can't lead without knowing what
   you're talking about. . . .
Third, the American legislative process is one of give and take.
   Use your power as a leader to persuade, not intimidate. . . .
Fourth, be considerate of the needs of your colleagues, even if
   they're at the bottom of the totem pole. . . .
                              —George Bush

(*See* Authority, Bosses, Character, Charisma, Command,
               Leadership [Personal], Power.)

Action

There comes a moment when you have to stop revving up the car
and shove it into gear.
                              —David Mahoney

If I had to sum up in one word what makes a good manager, I'd
say decisiveness. You can use the fanciest computers to gather the
numbers, but in the end you have to set a timetable and *act*.
                              —Lee J. Iacocca

Do not wait for ideal circumstances; they will never come; nor for
the best opportunities.
                              —Janet Erskine Stuart

I find the great thing in this world is not so much where we stand,
as in what direction we are moving: To reach the port of heaven,
we must sail sometimes with the wind and sometimes against it—
but we must sail, and not drift, nor lie at anchor.
                              —Oliver Wendell Holmes

Lead, follow, or get out of the way.
>   —Plaque on Ted Turner's desk

Leave a great talker in the middle of the street.
>   —English proverb

Leaders are problem solvers by talent and temperament, and by choice. For them, the new information environment—undermining old means of control, opening up old closets of secrecy, reducing the relevance of ownership, early arrival, and location—should seem less a litany of problems than an agenda for action. Reaching for a way to describe the entrepreneurial energy of his fabled editor Harold Ross, James Thurber said: "He was always leaning forward, pushing something invisible ahead of him." That's the appropriate posture for a knowledge executive.
>   —Harlan Cleveland

(*See* Decision-Making, Get Up and Go, Implementation, Performance, Progress.)

Advertising

To be heard afar, bang your gong on a hilltop.
>   —Chinese proverb

Seek for their predominant passion, or their prevailing weakness; and you will then know what to bait your hook with to catch them.
>   —Lord Chesterfield

The Chief Executive Officer should keep involved. The one thing that can make a spectacular difference in share points between competitors is advertising effectiveness. If the advertising agency feels strongly enough about an idea or a campaign and the marketing people are overly cautious, create an atmosphere where the disputed campaign can be shown to the CEO for final decision. Advertising should be created to move the ultimate boss, who is

the consumer. Try new things. Encourage your staff and the agency to look for the great idea. When it comes, the heavens open.
—Leo Greenland

Develop advertising as good as the product.
—Leo Burnett

I warn you against believing that advertising is a science. It is intuition and artistry, not science that develops effective advertising. . . .

Don't create at the expense of selling. . . . Establish a personality for the client's product. . . . Stand up to the client when convictions demand it. . . . You must have inventiveness but it must be disciplined. Everything you write, everything on a page, every word, every graphic symbol, every shadow should further the message you're trying to convey.
—William Bernbach

I want to get the exciter beams on their imaginations heated. So we draw and talk and write and talk until everyone internalizes the problem and adopts an intensely personal approach. Remember Raymond Rubicam's edict, "Resist the usual." The only way to achieve this is to pour a strategy through an individual so it comes out personal.
—Alexander Kroll

If you don't have anything to say, sing it.
—Advertising adage quoted by David Ogilvy

I advise: if you don't have anything to say, get a new creative team.
—Richard O'Neill

Yield to a man's tastes and he will yield to your interests.
—Edward Bulwer-Lytton

When a client proves refractory
Show a picture of his factory.

If he still moans and sighs
Make his logo twice the size.

But only in the direst cases
Ever show the client's faces.
    —Doggerel quoted in *Forbes*

When everyone but the C.E.O.
Keeps saying "yes" but he says "no,"
When he talks of Borman, Kiam and Lee,
And every other word is "me,"
When he says you've got just one more shot,
Put the client in the spot.
    —Allen G. Rosenshine

(*See* Truth in Advertising.)

Advisers

Commanders should be counseled, chiefly, by persons of known talent, by those who have made an art of war their particular study, and whose knowledge is derived from experience; from those who are present at the scene of action, who see the country, who see the enemy, who see the advantages that occasions offer, and who, like people embarked in the same ship, are sharers of the danger.
    —Lucius Aemilius Paulus
      Roman consul who led victorious
      campaign against the Macedonians

(*See* Headquarters Staff.)

Affectation

The first phase in the development of leadership, the first step toward the fast track, is to *stop pretending*, especially to ourselves,

that we are something that we are not. . . . Own up to our strengths and weaknesses. . . . Accept that we do not always operate at our highest levels. . . . Accept that we are where we are because of choices we have made in the past. . . . Accept that we do not fully control our destinies . . . live in the present and not in the past.
—Barbara A. Kovach

Don't affect the quality of calmness. It will give an appearance of false dignity which is only amusing.
—Erwin H. Schell

Affirmativeness

One should never think of death. One should think of life. That is real piety.
—Benjamin Disraeli

Aggressiveness

Transform the war into an offense on your part as soon as the occasion presents itself. All your maneuvers must lead toward this end.
—Frederick the Great

If the enemy leaves a door open, you must rush in.
—Sun Tzu

Be patiently aggressive.
—Edsel B. Ford II

In life you have to push yourself to the front of the line. . . . In the end stamina is what distinguishes you. No one leaves me behind.
—Robert Campeau

Drive thy business or it will drive thee.
—Benjamin Franklin

(*See* Boldness, Courage.)

Anticipation

Keeping a little ahead of conditions is one of the secrets of business; the trailer seldom goes far.
—Charles M. Schwab

Install systems that help you anticipate emerging issues and challenges. Value those working with or for you who have demonstrated an ability to anticipate.
—Arnold Brown and Edith Weiner

In Hiring:
The trick is to stay in touch, to keep your eyes and ears open, both to what you might need down the road and to who is or might be available. You don't want to get caught grabbing for anyone available at that last minute, because the last minute is not when you want to bring an unknown quantity on board.
—Merritt Sher

Argument

What convinces is conviction. Believe in the argument you're advancing. If you don't, you're as good as dead. The other person

will sense that something isn't there, and no chain of reasoning, no matter how logical or elegant or brilliant, will win your case for you.
                                —Lyndon B. Johnson

Don't take the wrong side of an argument just because your opponent has taken the right side.
                                —Baltasar Gracián

Use soft words and hard arguments.
                                —English proverb

When you have nothing to say, say nothing; a weak defence strengthens your opponent, and silence is less injurious than a weak reply.
                                —Charles Caleb Colton

In all Debates, let Truth be thy Aim, not Victory, or an unjust interest: And endeavor to gain, rather than to expose thy Antagonist.
                                —William Penn
                                Rules of Conversation

When a subject is highly controversial . . . one cannot hope to tell the truth. One can only show how one came to hold whatever opinion one does hold. One can only give one's audience the chance of drawing their own conclusions as they observe the limitations, the prejudices, the idiosyncrasies of the speaker.
                                — Virginia Woolf

(*See* Persuasion.)

Attitude

Adopt a stance with the head erect, neither hanging down, nor looking up, not twisted. Your forehead and the space between your eyes should not be wrinkled. Do not roll your eyes nor allow them to blink, but slightly narrow them. With your features composed, keep the line of your nose straight with a feeling of slightly flaring your nostrils.

—Miyamoto Musashi

[*Sprezzatura* ("unstudied nonchalance"):] Employ in everything a certain casualness which conceals art and creates the impression that what is done and said is accomplished without effort and without its being thought about. It is from this, in my opinion, that grace largely derives.

—Baldassare Castiglione
The Book of the Courtier, 1528

If a man be gloomy let him keep to himself. No one has a right to go croaking about society, or, what is worse, looking as if he stifled grief.

—Benjamin Disraeli

Let your Discourse with Men of Business be Short and Comprehensive.

—George Washington
Rules of Civility

(*See* Ego Trips, Hubris, Image.)

Authority

You do not lead by hitting people over the head—that's assault, not leadership.

—Dwight D. Eisenhower

Never give an order that can't be obeyed.

—General Douglas MacArthur

He makes a great mistake . . . who supposes that authority is firmer or better established when it is founded by force than that which is welded by affection.
                    —Terence

He who has great power should use it lightly.
                    —Seneca

(*See* Body Language, Bosses, Command, Leadership [Personal], Orders.)

B

Banker Relations

Never give up. The bankers and financial people did not take me seriously initially. Everyone thought I would fail. My attitude was that "No" is an unacceptable answer when it comes to financing.
—Debbi Fields

I visit our top bankers twice a year. You cannot call on these people only when you're in a jam. Handling crises is a hell of a lot easier if you've already got some rapport with the people who can help you solve them.
—Lee J. Iacocca

Bargaining

Drive a hard bargain, then make a liberal settlement. This always leaves the other man willing to do business.
—R. A. Long

Bargain like a gypsy, but pay like a gentleman.
—Hungarian proverb

Whenever you're sitting across from some important person, always picture him sitting there in a suit of long underwear. That's the way I always operated in business.
—Joseph P. Kennedy

Whenever you buy or sell, let or hire, make a definite bargain, and never trust to the flattering lie, "We shan't disagree about trifles."
—Charles Simmons

(*See* Negotiations.)

Big Picture

Don't equate activity with efficiency. You are paying your key people to see the big picture. Don't let them get bogged down in a lot of meaningless meetings and paper shuffling. Announce a Friday afternoon off once in a while. Cancel a Monday morning meeting or two. Tell the cast of characters you'd like them to spend the amount of time normally spent preparing for attending the meetings at their desks, simply thinking about an original idea.
—Harvey Mackay

It is not written in stone that the only function of a corporation is the purely economic one of maximizing short-term return for stockholders. You have to manage a company for its long-term growth and success.
—John Filer

Don't be afraid of maintaining an unsophisticated, childlike view. As Picasso said: "It takes a long time to grow young."
—Roy Rowan

"Surprises" are a cardinal sin. See each business situation for what it is and not through one's emotional glasses of what one might like to think it is. Make strategic planning a way of life.
—Reginald H. Jones

Body Language

. . . the great art of shaking hands: They were curious to know what this art was. I told them that if a man surrendered his arm to be shaken, by some horizontally, by others perpendicularly, and by others again with a strong grip, he could not fail to suffer severely from it, but that if he would *shake and not be shaken, grip and not be gripped,* taking care always to squeeze the hand of his adversary as hard as it squeezed him, then he suffered no inconvenience from it.
—President James K. Polk

Body language of authority: Become aware of body language. Your own and other people's. If you are explaining something important to your staff, try to convey some of your own urgency and enthusiasm; you'll diminish your effect if you're sitting rigidly, drawn tight together, with arms and legs crossed. . . . The body language that expresses confidence and authority is the easy, open stance, accompanied by direct eye contact with the other person. . . . If you stand up to address a seated person, you gain height and a certain amount of temporary power. But if you face the person directly, on his level (whether sitting or standing), you are more likely to establish communication.
—Cheryl Reimold

(*See* Authority.)

Boldness

Stow this talk. Care killed a cat. Fetch ahead for the doubloons.
                    —Long John Silver, in
                      Robert Louis Stevenson's
                      Treasure Island

No Captain can do very wrong if he places his ship alongside that of the enemy.
                    —Admiral Horatio Nelson

[Nelson's counsel] guided me time and again. On the eve of the critical battle of Santa Cruz, in which the Japanese ships outnumbered ours more than two to one, I sent my task force commanders this dispatch: ATTACK REPEAT ATTACK. They did attack, heroically, and when the battle was done, the enemy had turned away.

All problems, personal, national, or combat, become smaller if you don't dodge them, but confront them. Touch a thistle timidly, and it pricks you; grasp it boldly, and its spines crumble. Carry the battle to the enemy! Lay your ship alongside his!
                    —Admiral William F. "Bull" Halsey

> Tender-handed stroke a nettle
> And it stings you for your pains,
> Grasp it like a man of mettle,
> And it soft as silk remains.
>   —Aaron Hill (1685–1750)
>   "Words Written on a Window"

The moment one definitely commits oneself, then providence moves too. All sorts of things occur to help one that would never otherwise have occurred. A whole stream of events issues from the decision, raising in one's favor all manner of unforeseen incidents and meetings and material assistance which no man could have dreamed would have come his way. Whatever you can do or dream you can, begin it. Boldness has genius, power and magic in it. Begin it now.
                    —Attributed to Goethe

Never forget that no military leader has ever become great without audacity.
—Karl von Clausewitz

Don't be in awe of the President—talk back to him—few others will.
—Robert E. Merriam

(*See* Courage, Prudence, Resolution, Risk, Timidity.)

Borrowing

When a man is going to try to borrow money, it is wise to look prosperous.
—Benjamin Disraeli

Bosses

If you have a business, make sure that you're the one who's running it. If you don't want to accept the headaches of being boss, then either close the business down or sell it to someone who *will* accept the responsibilities.
—Advice favored by J. Paul Getty

The seven secrets of being a number one boss:
1. Develop professional expertise.
2. Sharpen your communication skills.
3. Cultivate enthusiasm.
4. Keep an open mind.
5. Pay attention to accomplishment.
6. Be accessible.

7. Respect your staff. (Treat your staff as you would your
   clients.)
                              —Cheryl Reimold

Remember the difference between a boss and a leader: a boss says
"Go!"—a leader says "Let's go!"
                              —Engine foreman E. M. Kelly

Define yourself by what you do, by how you treat others, and how
   they see you.
Define your business goals clearly so that others can see them as
   you do.
                              —George F. Burns

(*See* Authority, Goals, Inspiration, Leadership [Personal], Style.)

Boss/Secretary

The proper distance between boss and secretary: Never force her
to choose between her commitment to you and her duty to the
company. You have no right to expect her to throw herself on the
funeral pyre like a Hindu widow committing suicide.
                              —Anonymous CEO quoted by Mortimer
                                R. Feinberg and Aaron Levenstein

Bear in mind that no corporate business gift should ever be expensive, since it can then easily be misconstrued as a bribe. It is,
of course, always a bad idea to give your secretary a more expensive
gift than your wife, and an even worse idea to give anybody else
in the office a more expensive gift than you gave your secretary.
                              —Michael Korda

Tell the boss what you really think and the truth will set you free.
                              —Anon.

If you want to move up in business, the first rule is not to be invisible. . . . To be noticed by bosses, do ask questions and offer constructive advice. Don't substitute talk for action. Don't be afraid to present your best abilities when the opportunity arrives. Don't be shy.

—George Mazzei

Don't assume that the interests of employer and employee are necessarily hostile. . . . The opposite is more apt to be the case.

—Louis Dembitz Brandeis

Avoid outshining the master. . . . The stars in happy fashion teach us this lesson, for even though her children are bright, they are never so forward as to outshine the sun.

—Baltasar Gracián

If there's any single mistake that people make about holding on to their jobs, it's failure to communicate with the boss. I know the term "communication" is sometimes awkward, but I can't emphasize enough how important it is to let your boss know what you're doing.

—S. Eric Wachtel

Become a crucial subordinate, but don't become too valuable or you won't get promoted.

—Christine Hansen

Remember that the anger of the king is the messenger of death.

—Quintana

Better to ride on an ass that carries me, than an ass that throws me.

—Thomas Fuller

Be not too bold with your biggers or betters.

—English proverb

Bottom Line

If you're going to be an entrepreneur, in a corporation or on your own, you should get a background in accounting. . . . In so many ways, analysis of a profit and loss statement or cash flow can be useful. . . . Any bottom line is reached by addition and subtraction and is read in dollar signs and decimal points.
                              —Victor Kiam

Grow, grow, grow. Don't worry about profits, they'll come later.
                              —Donald C. Burr

It is no use saying "We are doing our best." You have got to succeed in doing what is necessary.
                              —Winston Churchill

Performance is your reality. Forget everything else.
                              —Harold Geneen

Look to the issue of things.
                              —English proverb

The new dimension that must be observed—a new "bottom line" for business, really—is social approval. Without it, economic victory would be Pyrrhic indeed.
                              —Thornton Bradshaw

Buck-Passing

One must never excuse oneself by pointing to the soldiers.
                              —Blaise Montluc

Do not lay on the multitude the blame that is due to a few.
                              —Ovid

Budgeting

Proportion your expenses to what you have, not what you expect.
> —English proverb

Be ruled by your purse.
> —English proverb

(*See* Cost Control.)

Bureaucracy

Never take a job that has no "in" box.
> —Henry Kissinger

If you're going to sin, sin against God, not the bureaucracy. God will forgive you but the bureaucracy won't.
> —Admiral Hyman G. Rickover

(*See* Red Tape.)

C

Capabilities

We must consult our means rather than our wishes, and not endeavor to better our affairs by attempting things, which, for want of success, may make them worse.
> —George Washington to Lafayette, 1780

To live happily with other people, ask of them only what they can give.
> —Tristan Bernard

(*See* Excellence, Proficiency.)

Change

Keep in mind that you can't control your own future. Your destiny is not in your hands; it is in the hands of the irrational consumer and society. The changes in their needs, desires, and demands will tell you where you must go. All this means that managers must

themselves feel the pulse of change on a daily, continuous basis. . . . They should have intense curiosity, observe events, analyze trends, seek the clues of change, and translate those clues into opportunities.
                                    —Michael J. Kami

Whosoever desires constant success must change his conduct with the times.
                                    —Niccolò Machiavelli

When a mature and able manager feels bored, he should seriously consider changing jobs, changing companies—or simply retiring. It is not fair to anyone for half a leader to hold a full-time leadership job.
                                    —James L. Hayes

Character

The forbearing use of power does not only form a touchstone; but the manner in which an individual enjoys certain advantages over others is a test of a *true gentleman*. The power which the strong have over the weak, the magistrate over the employed, the educated over the unlettered, the experienced over the confiding, even the clever over the silly; the forbearing and inoffensive use of all this power or authority, or a total abstinence from it, when the case admits it, will show the gentleman in a plain light. The gentleman does not needlessly and unnecessarily remind an offender of a wrong he may have committed against him. He can only forgive; he can forget; and he strives for that nobleness of self and mildness of character which imparts sufficient strength to let the past be but the past.
                                    —General Robert E. Lee

Charisma

In *The Edge of the Sword* de Gaulle wrote that a leader "must be able to create a spirit of confidence in those under him. He must be able to assert his authority." Authority, de Gaulle argued, derives from prestige, and prestige "is largely a matter of feeling, suggestion and impression, and it depends primarily on the possession of an elementary gift, a natural attitude" . . . lately gone by the fashionable term charisma. . . . To this ineffable quality, de Gaulle wrote, a leader must add three concrete ones: mystery, character, and grandeur. "First and foremost," he declared, "there can be no prestige without mystery, for familiarity breeds contempt. All religions have their tabernacles, and no man is a hero to his valet."
                                   —Richard Nixon

Beware of charisma . . . "Representative Men" was Ralph Waldo Emerson's 1850 phrase for the great men in a democracy. . . . Is there some common quality among these Representative Men who have been most successful as our leaders? I call it the need to be *authentic*—or, as our dictionaries tell us, "conforming to fact and therefore worthy of trust, reliance or belief." While the charismatic has an uncanny outside source of strength, the authentic is strong because he is what he seems to be.
                                   —Daniel J. Boorstin

Throw away those books and cassettes on inspirational leadership. Send those consultants packing. Know your job, set a good example for the people under you and put results over politics. That's all the charisma you'll really need to succeed.
                                   —Dyan Machan

(*See* Mystery.)

Chemistry (Personal)

Never hire anyone who is going to report directly to you who you do not intuitively just plain like from first impressions. If you don't have that sort of comfortable chemistry going you are going to end up wasting hours deciding which side of a stamp to lick. You may think you can work things through for the good of the company with someone with whom you don't have good rapport but at the start of the company you can't afford to waste time working things through. If your instincts tell you you're going to have a hard time working with someone, pass.

—Fred Charette

Clarity

Give orders that are clear and strong. Admiral Nimitz had the great fortune of receiving unambiguous instructions. Roosevelt to Knox, Secretary of the Navy, Dec. 16, 1941: "Tell Nimitz to get the hell to Pearl and stay there until the war is over."

—Edward N. Luttwak

When all is said and done the greatest quality required in a commander is "decision"; he must be able to issue clear orders and have the drive to get things done. Indecision and hesitation are fatal in any officer; in a C-in-C they are criminal.

—Viscount Montgomery of Alamein

(*See* Obedience, Orders, Writing.)

Comeback

If you stand up and be counted, from time to time you may get yourself knocked down. But remember this: A man flattened by an opponent can get up again. A man flattened by conformity stays down for good.
— Thomas J. Watson, Jr.

Command

One week before the opening battle [in Northern Tunisia] Eisenhower had counseled me to be tough with the division commanders. "As a final word," he said, "let me offer you one item of advice. It is that you must be tough. You must be tough with your immediate commanders and they must be equally tough with their respective subordinates. We have passed the time where we cannot demand from troops reasonable results after you have made careful plans and preparations and estimated that the task can be accomplished. . . ." However . . . toughness alone is not enough. The corps commander must know his division commanders, he must thoroughly understand their problems, respect their judgment, and be tolerant of their limitations. . . . Success comes . . . from a well-balanced combination of good judgment, self-confidence, leadership and boldness.
— General Omar N. Bradley

(See Tough-Mindedness.)

Committees

If you ever live in a country run by a committee, be on the committee.
>—William Graham Sumner

Having served on various committees I have drawn up a list of rules: Never arrive on time; this stamps you as a beginner. Don't say anything until the meeting is half over; this stamps you as wise. Be as vague as possible; this avoids irritating the others. When in doubt, suggest a subcommittee be appointed. Be the first to move for adjournment; this will make you popular; it's what everyone is waiting for.
>—Harry Chapman

Say as little as possible while appearing to be awake.
>—William P. Rogers

Measure not dispatch by the times of sitting, but by the advancement of the business.
>—Sir Francis Bacon

There is no more dangerous citizen than the person with a gift of gab, a crusading complex and a determination "to pass a law" as the antidote for all human ills. The most effective diversion of such an individual . . . is to associate him on research committees with a few persons who have a passion for truth. . . . I can now disclose the secret that I created a dozen committees for that precise purpose.
>—Herbert Hoover

You can't build a strong corporation with a lot of committees and a board that has to be consulted at every turn. You have to be able to make decisions on your own.
>—Rupert Murdoch

If you're pestered by critics and
hounded by faction,

To take some precipitate, positive
    action,
The proper procedure, to take my
    advice, is
Appoint a commission and stave off
    the crisis.
                —Punch

Communication

Frown on lapses of information. When people admit that they didn't keep you informed, let them know that you don't want this kind of "protection." A couple of strong reactions by the manager, and a subordinate learns to make sure the boss gets the word—all of it.
                —Thomas L. Quick

Keep things informal. Talking is the natural way to do business. Writing is great for keeping records and putting down details, but talk generates ideas. Great things come from our luncheon meetings which consist of a sandwich, a cup of soup, and a good idea or two. No martinis.
                —T. Boone Pickens

On telephone answering machines:
Don't complain about having to talk to a machine. Don't talk to the machine. ("Hi, Allison's machine. Good to hear your voice. Tell your owner I called, will you?") And don't hang up unless your intention is to exasperate rather than communicate.
           —Glen Waggoner and Kathleen Maloney

The commander must be at constant pains to keep his troops abreast of all the latest tactical experience and developments, and must insist on their practical application. He must see to it that his subordinates are trained in accordance with the latest require-

ments. The best form of "welfare" for the troops is first-class train-
ing, for this saves unnecessary casualties.
—Field Marshal Erwin Rommel

Competition

Don't fight a battle if you don't gain anything by winning.
—General George S. Patton, Jr.

Let a man contend to the uttermost
For his life's set prize, be it what it will!
—Robert Browning

Don't sit around with competitors and agree that there's plenty of
business to go around. Try to get good enough to deserve all the
business, his too. . . . The prerequisite of success is survival, or
as they say in Las Vegas, you'll never win craps if you're not at
the table.
—Richard W. Wilcke

Thou shalt not covet; but tradition
Approves all forms of competition.
—Arthur Hugh Clough

Compete, don't envy.
—Moroccan proverb

Competition is easier to accept if you realize it is not an act of
aggression or abrasion. . . . I've worked with my best friends in
direct competition. Whatever you want in life, other people are
going to want, too. Believe in yourself enough to accept the idea
that you have an equal right to it.
—Diane Sawyer

Never press the competition beyond a certain reasonable limit.
—David J. Rogers

Grasp the possibility that a truly tough and worthy competitor knows not only how to fight but also when to quit.
            —Jeffrey Z. Rubin

In your dealings with competitors and opponents, try not to be predictable. This will add to your power, as other people will spend time trying to figure out what you're likely to do.
            —Herb Schmertz

Always go before our enemies with confidence, otherwise our apparent uneasiness inspires them with greater boldness.

Do not fight too often with one enemy, or you will teach him all your art of war.
            —Napoleon I

Do not despise the enemy who looks small.
            —Japanese proverb

Let not him who is houseless pull down the house of another; but let him labor diligently and build one for himself.
            —Abraham Lincoln

Always remember the other guy's got to make a buck too. If you don't leave him a profitable option, you'll hit his hot button. I'm surprised how many people think you can throw a hand grenade at a competitor and expect he'll stand there and enjoy it.
            —Frank Lorenzo

Never do card tricks for the group you play poker with.
            —Anon.

(*See* Opponents.)

Complacency

Who feels no ills,
Should, therefore, fear them; and when fortune smiles,
Be doubly cautious, lest destruction come
Remorseless on him, and he fall unpitied.
                                —Sophocles

Let not sloth dim your honors new begot.
                        —Messenger, in Shakespeare's
                        1 *Henry VI*

Never rest on your oars as a boss. If you do, the whole company
starts sinking.
                                —Lee J. Iacocca

Never shrink from doing anything which your business calls you
to do. The man who is above his business may one day find his
business above him.
                                —Drew

Run scared . . . and they never catch you.
                                —Joan Rivers

Compromise

Appreciate and develop the art of compromise in your lifestyle.
Keep true to your goals and values, but give yourself some operating room. Understand that you often have to work a long time
to achieve your goals, and the steps to success are often small ones.
                                —Win Borden

Even when one compromises, one should never compromise in regard to the basic truth.

—Jawaharlal Nehru

Compromise is usually bad. It should be a last resort. If two departments or a division have a problem they can't solve and it comes to you, listen to both sides and then, unlike Solomon, pick one or the other. This places solid responsibility on the winner to make it work.

—Robert Townsend

Better bend than break.

—Scottish proverb

Where there is no choice, we do well to make no difficulty.

—George Macdonald

Computer Etiquette

Don't Leave People Holding the Phone Indefinitely While Commanding Your Computer: Putting people on hold for more than 30 seconds after telling them you have to find their file in your computer is enough to get anyone teed off, especially if they're paying for the phone call. If you have a text retrieval program, your job is made easier, because you can search automatically while you chat with the person about the weather. Otherwise, you'll be scanning subdirectories yourself, calling up a file and aborting it, calling up another, trying to jog your not-infallible memory. If the thumb-thumping on the other end becomes too loud, tell them you'll call them back once you find the file.

—*Personal Computing* magazine

Concealment

Should'st thou unhappily be inclin'd to be covetous, given to women, or a glutton, as I hope thou art not, avoid shewing thy self guilty of those vices; for when the town, and those that come near thee have discover'd thy weakness, they'll be sure to try thee on that side, and tempt thee to thy everlasting ruin.
　　　　　　—Cervantes

Concentration of Forces

Never concentrate your forces at a point that isn't valuable to you even if the opponent is weak there. Going for the thinnest place in the hedge makes good sense only if what's on the other side of the hedge appeals to you.
　　　　　　—David J. Rogers

It is better to be on hand [at the decisive point] with ten men than to be absent with ten thousand.
　　　　　　—Tamerlane

I always make it a rule to get there first with the most men.
　　　　　　—General Nathan Bedford Forrest
　　　　　　(Widely misquoted as "I git thar
　　　　　　fustest with the mostest men.")

Concentration is the secret of strength in politics, in war, in trade, in short in all management of human affairs.
　　　　　　—Ralph Waldo Emerson

The essence of strategy is, with a weaker army, always to have more force at the crucial point than the enemy.
　　　　　　—Napoleon I

March divided and fight concentrated.
                    —Military maxim

(*See* Offensive Strategy.)

Confidants

I can understand that you wonder why I need that half-man around me.* But—some day you may well be sitting here where I am now as President of the United States. And when you are, you'll be looking at that door over there and knowing that practically everybody who walks through it wants something out of you. You'll learn what a lonely job this is, and you'll discover the need for somebody like Harry Hopkins, who asks for nothing except to serve you.
                    —Franklin D. Roosevelt, quoted by
                    Robert Sherwood

*The harsh reference was to Hopkins' physical frailty.

Do you really want to know what the present President of the United States lacks and *must* have, if he is to serve his country as he should and give the best that is in him to his tasks? He needs *pleasure* and the unaffected human touch! He cannot live on duty. He cannot feed his heart on "great questions." He must have the constant tonic of personal friendships, old and sweet and tested, that have nothing to do with him as a politician.
                    —Woodrow Wilson

(*See* Advisers, Family Values, Fun, Headquarters Staff.)

Confidence

Stand up. Look 'em in the eye, and tell 'em what you know.
> —Dan Rather, quoting his mother's
> advice

Have enough confidence in yourself to let the other fellow take some risk.
> —General Electric Corp. aphorism
> quoted by Robert J. Buckley

Trust men and they will be true to you; treat them greatly and they will show themselves great.
> —Ralph Waldo Emerson

Trust him with little, who, without proofs, trusts you with everything.
> —Johann Kaspar Lavater

Let the captain show that he himself is lighthearted, and full of hope by means of his facial expression, his words and his dress. His visage should be severe, his eyes intrepid and luminous, and his clothing flamboyant. He should banter with his men, be clever and witty. They will then deduce that their general could not jest and enjoy himself like that if there were any real danger, if he did not think that he was much stronger or if he did not have good reason to scorn the enemy. The troops are bound to take confidence.
> —Raimondo Montecuccoli
> Imperial General
> of the Thirty Years War

Some guys, in order to get their attention, you have to holler at them and fine them. There are other guys you can't. Some guys you holler at them, they crawl into a shell. Some guys you holler at them, they lose their confidence. You gotta always try to do everything you can to help them maintain that confidence level.
> —Tommy Lasorda

And too much confidence:
Let him that thinketh he standeth take heed lest he fall.
                              —I Corinthians 10:12

(*See* Self-Esteem.)

Contacts

Be aware that an upright minister asks *what* recommends a man; a corrupt minister, *who?*
                              —Charles Caleb Colton

(*See* Evaluation.)

Contracts

When a friend deals with a friend, let the bargain be clear and well penn'd, that they may continue friends to the end.

Beware! Beware! He'll cheat without scruple, who can without fear.
                              —Benjamin Franklin

Drink nothing without seeing it; sign nothing without reading it.
                              —Spanish proverb

When you go to buy, use your eyes, not your ears.
                              —Czech proverb

Though negotiations are a rough game, you should never allow them to become a dirty game. Once you've agreed to a deal, don't back out of it unless the other party fails to deliver as promised. Your handshake is your bond. As far as I'm concerned, a handshake

is worth more than a signed contract. As an entrepreneur, a reputation for integrity is your most valuable commodity. If you try to put something over on someone, it will come back to haunt you.
—Victor Kiam

(*See* Negotiating.)

Contrarianism

If you defy the system long enough you'll be rewarded. At first life takes revenge and reduces you to a sniveling mess. But keep sniveling, have the madness, the audacity, to do what interests you, forget about your person, and eventually life will say all right, we'll let you do it.
—Jo Coudert

My central principle of investment is to go contrary to general opinion, on the ground that, if everyone is agreed about its merits, the investment is inevitably too dear and therefore unattractive.
—John Maynard Keynes

Go against the grain.
—Arthur Gray, Jr.

Do not choose to be wrong for the sake of being different.
—Lord Samuel

Control

Work constantly at gaining and maintaining the consent of those who work for you. In years to come, authority to govern will increasingly flow from below as the work force continues to become

more educated, more highly skilled, and more concerned with individual feelings of control.
                    —Arnold Brown and Edith Weiner

The struggle among competing interests always has a high claim on the attention of leadership. . . . In exercising control, leadership has a dual task. It must *win* the consent of constituent units, in order to maximize voluntary cooperation, and, therefore, must permit emergent interest blocs a wide degree of representation. At the same time, in order to hold the helm, it must see that a balance of power appropriate to the fulfillment of key commitments will be maintained.
                    —Philip Selznick

There's an old saw that says, "You can't delegate a haircut." . . . No chief executive can delegate responsibility for control. "Controls," yes, but not control. The financial officer or controller can and should master the controls needed for effective operating management, but the kind of control that determines where an organization fits into society, what its future will be, and what will happen to its people—that's the CEO's hair.
                    —James L. Hayes

Don't "over-control" like a novice pilot. Stay loose enough from the flow that you can observe it, modify, and improve it.
                    —Donald H. Rumsfeld

(*See* Delegating Authority, Empowerment, Leadership [Personal].)

Conventions

If you are No. 1, be first: When you run the convention, be the first one to arrive at all meetings and social events and the first to leave. You create an attitude that is businesslike in a setting that rarely is. Most conventions are set amid exotic flora and fauna, and

if you want to keep the conventioneers on target, it is wise not to
be the last to come to the events and the last to leave the bar.
—Lois Wyse

(*See* Delegating Authority.)

Cooling Off Period

We are told, "Let not the sun go down on your wrath": but I would
add, never act or write till it has done so. This rule has saved me
from many an act of folly. It is wonderful what a different view we
take of the same event four-and-twenty hours after it has happened.
—Sydney Smith

Coolness Under Fire

One of the first rules of playing the power game is that all bad
news must be accepted calmly, as if one already knew and didn't
much care.
—Michael Korda

The first quality for a commander-in-chief is a cool head to receive
a correct impression of things. He should not allow himself to be
confused by either good or bad news.
—Napoleon I

Corporate Giving

If thou art rich, then show the greatness of thy fortune; or what is better, the greatness of thy soul . . . support the distressed, and patronize the neglected. Be great; but let it be in considering riches as they are, as talents committed to an earthen vessel. Thou art but the receiver.
—Laurence Stern

[The prince] ought to produce festivals and shows; he should recognize different classes and guilds and from time to time mingle with them, to show his humanity and munificence. He should always uphold, however, his humanity and dignity.
—Niccolò Machiavelli

Let us not paralyze our capacity for good by brooding over man's capacity for evil.
—David Sarnoff

Never respect men merely for their riches, but rather for their philanthropy; we do not value the sun for its height, but for its use.
—Gamaliel Bailey

Write injuries in dust, benefits in marble.
—Benjamin Franklin

(*See* Philanthropy.)

Corruption

. . . while foreign custom may be enlisted as an explanation for particular improprieties, it is quite unreliable as a general defense of multinational behavior. . . . The "trivial" case of grease money,

then, should be seen as the top of a very slippery slope. Once you let a single corrupt official, working under the aegis of "custom," rearrange your business ethics for you, you are wed to moral submissiveness as long as you do business in his country.
—Tad Tuleja

(*See* Mafia Connections.)

Cost Control

Here is a piece of advice
That is worth a king's crown:
To hold your head up,
Hold your overhead down.
—Ruth Boostin

In the field of cost control, use your budget as a tool to be placed in your foremen's hands—not as a club to be held over their heads.
—James L. Pierce

The executive must always be ready to supply a pinch of unwarranted optimism into the stew of calculated costs.
—Harlan Cleveland

The only truly effective way to cut costs is to cut out an activity altogether. To try to cut back costs is rarely effective. There is little point in trying to do cheaply what should not be done at all.
—Peter F. Drucker

(*See* Budgeting.)

Courage

Only be thou strong, and very courageous, then thou shalt make thy way prosperous, and then thou shalt have good success.
—Joshua 1:7,8

Whatever your sex or position, life is a battle in which you are to show your pluck, and woe be to the coward. Whether passed on a bed of sickness or a tented field, it is ever the same fair play and admits no foolish distinction. Despair and postponement are cowardice and defeat. Men were born to succeed, not to fail.
—Henry David Thoreau

Fight hard when you are down; die hard—determine at least to do—and you won't die at all.
—James H. West

(*See* Boldness.)

Credibility

Protect your own credibility. . . . One of the highest—and most beneficial—accolades for a manager is the comment, "If he says so, you can bank on it."
—James L. Hayes

"I might have my hand full of truth," said the French poet Fontanelle once, "and open only my little finger." But the truth had better really be firmly held in that hand. Even more important, that hand had better be clean and always in sight. Political sleight of hand is what has cost Presidents their credibility.
—Brock Brower

There is one cardinal principle which must always be remembered: one must never make a show of false emotions to one's men. The ordinary soldier has a surprisingly good nose for what is true and what false.

—Field Marshal Erwin Rommel

(*See* Honesty, Performance, Truth in Advertising.)

Creeds

Do more than exist—live.
Do more than touch—feel.
Do more than look—observe.
Do more than read—absorb.
Do more than hear—listen.
Do more than listen—understand.

—John H. Rhoades,
quoted by Paul O. Sand

Earn from the powerful, favor; from the active and good, advancement; from the many, affection; from the individual, love.

—Goethe

If you are lost—"climb, conserve and confess." (From the Navy SNJ Flight Manual.)

—Donald H. Rumsfeld

Criticism

Never giving criticism without praise is a strict rule for me. No matter what you are criticizing, you must find something good to say—both *before* and *after*. . . . Criticize the act, not the person.

—Mary Kay Ash

The only graceful way to accept an insult is to ignore it; if you can't ignore it, top it; if you can't top it, laugh at it; if you can't laugh at it, it's probably deserved.
                    —Russell Lynes

Reprove a friend in secret but praise him before others.
                    —Leonardo da Vinci

Always decry the time in which you live; it is a proof of vitality.
                    —Hilaire Belloc

Knock somebody in the head. If not an actor, then the author, and if not the author, then the manager. . . . But make it hearty, make it hot. You must give a good show, and a good show means one with slaughter in it.
                    —H. L. Mencken

Never trust the artist. Trust the tale. The proper function of a critic is to save the tale from the artist who created it.
                    —D. H. Lawrence

Whatever course you decide upon, there is always some one to tell you you are wrong. There are always difficulties arising which tempt you to believe that your critics are right. To map out a course of action and follow it to the end, requires some of the same courage which a soldier needs. Peace has its victories, but it takes brave men to win them.
                    —Ralph Waldo Emerson

Capitalize upon criticism. It's one of the hardest things in the world to accept criticism, especially when it's not presented in a constructive way, and turn it to your advantage.
                    —J. C. Penney

Hanlon's razor: Never attribute to malice that which is adequately explained by stupidity.
                    —Arthur Bloch

[On criticizing a subordinate:] Get to the point. Don't evade the issue. Skip the small talk and go straight to the target: "Bob, I want to talk to you about your late reports"; or "Barbara, I called you in to discuss your personality conflict with the director of sales." . . . Stalling and beating about the bush usually only increase the anxieties on both sides. . . . Encourage the subordinate to tell his side of the story. . . . Agree on the source of the problem and its solution.

—J. Stephen Morris

Don't make tragedies of trifles,
Don't shoot butterflies with rifles—
Laugh it off!
—Anon.

(*See* Praises, Reprimand.)

Cutting Losses

Never become mired in defending an unworkable idea out of some misguided ego or machismo motivation. Cut your losses and move on.

—James C. Freund

Do not persist in folly. Some make it a duty of failure and having started down the wrong road, think it is a badge of character to continue.

—Baltasar Gracián

If you have made a mistake, cut your losses as quickly as possible.
—Bernard M. Baruch

We ought not to stretch either our legs or our hopes for a point they cannot reach.
—Epictetus

(*See* Profit and Loss.)

D

Deception

All warfare is based on deception. Therefore, when capable, feign incapacity; when active, inactivity. When near, make it appear that you are far away; when far away, that you are near. Offer the enemy a bait to lure him; feign disorder and strike him. When he concentrates, prepare against him; where he is strong, avoid him. Anger his general and confuse him. Pretend inferiority and encourage his arrogance.
— Sun Tzu

There is required for the composition of a great commander not only massive common sense and reasoning power, not only imagination, but also an element of legerdemain, an original and sinister touch, which leaves the enemy puzzled as well as beaten.
— Winston Churchill

In large-scale strategy, when you cannot see the enemy's position, indicate that you are about to attack strongly, to discover his resources. It is easy then to defeat him with a different method once you see his resources.

In large-scale strategy we can use our troops to confuse the enemy on the field. Observing the enemy's spirit, we can make him think,

"Here? There? Like that? Like this? Slow? Fast?" Victory is certain when the enemy is caught up in a rhythm which confuses the spirit.
—Miyamoto Musashi

Concealment of intentions is of the utmost importance in order to provide surprise for one's own operations and thus make it possible to exploit the time taken by the enemy command to react. Deception measures of all kinds should be encouraged, if only to make the enemy commander uncertain and cause him to hesitate and hold back.
—Field Marshal Erwin Rommel

(*See* Offensive Strategy.)

Decision-Making

All my life whenever it comes time to make a decision, I make it and forget about it, and go to work on something else, and when these things came before me, as President of the United States, I made the decision on them, and went into the next thing. You never have time to stop. You've got to keep going because there's always a decision just ahead of you that you've got to make, and you don't want to look back. If you make a mistake in one of these decisions, correct it by another decision, and go ahead.
—Harry S. Truman

Harry, never display agony in public, in an opinion. Never display agony. Never say this is an agonizing, difficult decision. Always write it as though it's as clear as crystal.
—Justice Hugo Black to Justice Harry
Blackmun

Don't be afraid when you have no other choice.
—Yiddish proverb

[The "ideal" White House decision-making process should encompass:] . . . first: agreement on the facts; second: agreement on the

overall policy objective; third: a precise definition of the problem; fourth: a canvassing of all possible solutions, with all their shades and variations; fifth: a list of all the possible consequences that would flow from each solution; sixth: a recommendation and final choice of one alternative; seventh: the communication of that selection; and eighth: provision for its execution.
                                        —Theodore Sorensen

Accept rigorous debate, and then make a decision. You're the one who has to do it; you can't just hope it will evolve by some mystical group process.
                                        —Abraham Zaleznik

When, against one's will, one is high-pressured into making a hurried decision, the best answer is always "No," because "No" is more easily changed to "Yes" than "Yes" is changed to "No."
                                        —Charles E. Nielsen

[On the importance of disagreement:] Gentlemen, I take it we are all in complete agreement on the decision here. [Nods of assent.] Then I propose we postpone further discussion of this matter until our next meeting to give ourselves time to develop disagreement and perhaps gain some understanding of what the decision is all about.
                                        —Attributed to Alfred P. Sloan, Jr.

Be willing to make decisions. That's the most important quality in a good leader. Don't fall victim to what I call the "ready-aim-aim-aim-aim syndrome." You must be willing to fire.
                                        —T. Boone Pickens

I have an absolute rule. I refuse to make a decision that somebody else can make. The first rule of leadership is to save yourself for the big decision. Don't allow your mind to become cluttered with the trivia. Don't let yourself become the issue.
                                        —Richard Nixon

On indecision:
Don't fight the problem. Decide it!
                                        —General George C. Marshall

While trout fishing at my country home, my friend John McCloy told me that when he was running Germany, as Allied High Commissioner, he always asked himself a few basic questions before making any decision.
1. Does it make sense?
2. Is it fair?

—John Diebold

If you wait to make an important decision until all the information that you might want is in, you will never make it in time. Depending on the risks, on what the stakes are, you have to settle for 75, 70, or 65 percent of the information that you need. And on the basis of what you have, make your decision and go, because the time and the cost of getting, say, the last 25 percent are not commensurate with what you might gain by deferring the decision.

—Paraphrase of a rule of Harold Geneen

When a decision has been made and the die is cast, then murder the alternatives.

—Mrs. Emory S. Adams, Jr.,
quoted by Dorothy Sarnoff

(*See* Action.)

Dedication

To do something better, you must work an extra bit harder. I like the phrase an *extra bit harder*. For me it is not just a slogan, but a habitual state of mind, a disposition. Any job one takes on must be grasped and felt with one's soul, mind and heart; only then will one work an extra bit harder.

—Mikhail Gorbachev

Age quid agis, says the Latin: Do what you do. Be in earnest, and do not trifle.

—C. H. Spurgeon

You have to invest yourself. There are no nine-to-five possibilities in terms of true success in business or the professions. Dedication is the key.
—Jack Hilton

To sense the potential of posterity in one's daily business life, one has to feel deeply about some aspect of one's work. One has to be committed to do or create something that will accomplish some good in this world. . . . The key ingredients are dedication to a profound idea and the determination to carry it out.
—David Finn

Go forward, forward—even unto death.
—Mustapha al-Barzani

"You have to put your heart in the business and the business in your heart." So goes the old maxim, no better exemplified than in the story of crusty James Gordon Bennett, who stalked into the office of his *New York Herald* at the same moment that a young copy boy dashed around a corner. The collision sent Bennett sprawling on the floor. "Young man," he roared, "what in blazes do you think you're doing!" The kid stammered: "I was just running an errand, sir," Bennett put his hand in his pocket, flipped him a quarter and snapped: "Well, that's the way to run 'em!"
—Edward Bleier

(*See* Hard Work.)

Deference

When you have a strong ego, and the strength to use your power, you learn by experience that it is best in life to listen to people who can help you make a decision, and to *defer* to people, sometimes against your better judgment, because you've learned by experience that it's wise to defer to them for any number of reasons. Then you go home in the evening with this gnawing feeling in your

insides, asking yourself, "Am I abdicating my responsibilities, am I reduced to the role of an arbiter? Why am I not that strong chief executive? Maybe I'm just a weakling."
                    —W. Michael Blumenthal

Delegating Authority

This thing is too heavy for thee; thou art not able to perform it thyself alone. . . . Be thou for the people to God-ward . . . and thou shalt teach them statutes and the laws, and shalt shew them the way wherein they must walk, and the work they must do. Moreover thou shalt provide out of all the people able men, such as fear God, men of truth, hating unjust gain, and place such over them, to be rulers of thousands, and rulers of hundreds, rulers of fifties and rulers of tens; and let them judge the people of all seasons . . . and they shalt bear the burden with thee. . . . If thou shalt do this thing, and God command thee so, then thou shalt be able to endure. . . . So Moses hearkened to the voice of his father in law, and did all that he had said.
                    —Jethro's advice to Moses,
                    Exodus 18:17–25

You will certainly not be able to take the lead in all things yourself. To one man a God has given deeds of war, and to another the dance, to another the lyre and song, and in another wide-sounding Zeus puts a good mind.
                    —Homer

Do not put a sword into a madman's hand.
                    —English proverb

Because a thing seems difficult for you, do not think it impossible for anyone to accomplish.
                    —Marcus Aurelius

Do pleasant things yourself, but unpleasant things through others.
                    —Baltasar Gracián

Delegate to the one with the most to lose
And not to the one with the most to gain.
—Anon.

When Secretary of Defense Charles E. Wilson bothered [Eisenhower] too often with details, Ike was blunt: "Look here, Charlie, I want *you* to run Defense. We *both* can't run it, and I *won't* run it. I was elected to worry about a lot of things other than the day-to-day operations of a department."
—James David Barber

I neither ask nor desire to know anything of your plans. Take the responsibility and act, and call on me for assistance.
—Abraham Lincoln to General Ulysses
S. Grant on his appointment to
command the Union armies, 1864

It's great to be an entrepreneur and provide direction. But when you get big enough you've got to delegate. Believe me, I learned the hard way.
—Donald C. Burr

You can delegate authority, but you can never delegate responsibility for delegating a task to someone else. If you picked the right man, fine, but if you picked the wrong man, the responsibility is yours—not his.
—Richard A. Krafve

(*See* Control, Conventions, Orders, Power.)

Determination

A man is to go about his business as if he had not a friend in the world to help him in it.
—Lord Halifax

Never say die.
> —Charles Dickens

Sports mimics business in many ways. If you want to be as good or better than anyone else, you better be as fit as them. And when you're fit and talented, [it is] determination that differentiates the good player from the great player.
> —Anthony J. F. O'Reilly

Just keep going. Everybody gets better if they keep at it.
> —Ted Williams

You've got to get up every morning with determination if you're going to go to bed with satisfaction.
> —George Horace Lorimer

The test of a first-rate intelligence is the ability to hold two opposed ideas in the mind at the same time, and still retain the ability to function. One should, for example, be able to see that things are hopeless and yet be determined to make them otherwise.
> —F. Scott Fitzgerald

Never go backward. Attempt, and do it with all your might. Determination is power.
> —Charles Simmons

(*See* Perseverance, Playing to Win.)

Diplomacy

In contrast to the suave and amiable Eisenhower, [General Bedell] Smith could be blunt and curt. Yet like his chief, he was articulate and expressive, sophisticated, and discreet during those diplomatic crises that occasionally erupted at SHAEF. "Bedell, tell them to go to hell," Eisenhower once said in referring to a mission to SHAEF, "but put it so they won't be offended."
> —General Omar N. Bradley

Cease firing, but if any enemy planes appear, shoot them down in a friendly fashion.

> —Admiral William F. "Bull" Halsey
> Message to Third Fleet at sea off
> Tokyo after receipt of word of Japanese
> surrender, August 15, 1945

(*See* Tact.)

Directors

The chief executive officer who avoids using directors as overseers of management performance is acting unwisely, if not imprudently. Presidents and other top-echelon managers may use the board as a voice of conscience, a control mechanism, a sounding board, or an endorsing agent—but they *should* use it.

> —James L. Hayes

Poison pills give shareholders the right to buy shares at a special price, or to receive some other benefit, when a hostile bidder tries to take over the company. . . . However, a board of directors may fear that a poison pill sometimes will depress the price of the company's shares. Hence there is risk in adopting such a plan. To put a board of directors in a proper frame of mind, one Wall Street adviser would begin his presentation of a pill with the story of two men who are walking in the woods and who suddenly see a big grizzly bear coming at them. One of them takes off his knapsack, takes out his running shoes, unlaces his hiking boots, and starts putting on his running shoes. The other says, "Dummy, you can't outrun that bear." The first replies, "I don't have to outrun the bear, I only have to outrun you."

> —Arthur Fleischer, Jr., Geoffrey C.
> Hazard, Jr., and Miriam Z. Klipper

Discipline

Some players you pat their butts, some players you kick their butts, some players you leave alone.
—Pete Rose

Discipline is not made to order, cannot be created offhand; it is a matter of tradition. The Commander must have absolute confidence in his right to command, must have the habit of command, pride in commanding.
—Ardant du Picq

We should not pity or pardon those who have yielded to great temptation, or, perchance, great provocation. Besides, it is right that our sympathies should be kept for the injured.
—Benjamin Disraeli

Morale is one of the most elusive concepts that a manager has to deal with, and it is one that can easily lead the manager astray. It is usually mixed up with the debate as to the better way to run a company . . . as a "taut ship" or as a "happy ship." My experience and observation tell me that the taut ship, with high standards fairly administered, is always the happiest.
—Louis B. Lundborg

Never coddle a malcontent.
—Peter Baida

Now these are the Laws of the Jungle
and many and mighty are they;
But the head and the hoof of the Law
and the haunch and the hump is
—Obey!
—Rudyard Kipling

(*See* Obedience.)

Downsizing

We've got to be sure we don't create organizations with a CEO at the top, a computer in the middle, and lots of workers at the bottom.
—Robert T. Tomasko

(*See* Organization.)

Dress

Observe the shining part of every man of fashion, who is liked and esteemed; attend to and imitate that particular accomplishment for which you hear him chiefly celebrated and distinguished; then collect those various parts, and make yourself a mosaic of the whole. No one body possesses every thing, and almost every body possesses some one thing, worthy of imitation.
—Lord Chesterfield

(*See* Image.)

Drug Testing

Never learn anything about your men except from themselves. A good manager needs no detectives, and the fellow who can't read human nature can't manage it.
—George Horace Lorimer

If you suspect a man, don't employ him, and if you employ him, don't suspect him.
—Chinese proverb

E

Ego Trips

Let no one think he has been anointed as the Savior.
—Goethe

No put yourself in a barrel when match box can hol' you.
—Jamaican proverb

Seem not greater than thou art.
—English proverb

Don't be proud of dumb things. It's dumb to be proud of production records rather than products. It's dumb to be proud of a plant rather than the working conditions of your employees. It's dumb to flaunt your wealth and then try to tell employees that times are tough, vacations must be cancelled, etc. It's dumb to ask employees to make any sacrifice you are not willing to make in kind.
—Lois Wyse

(*See* Attitude, Hubris, Humility, Image.)

Empowerment

Today's leaders have what I call the power to "empower" others.
The author Henry Miller expressed this concept best when he
wrote:

> "No one is great enough or wise enough for any of us to
> surrender our destiny to. The only way in which anyone can
> lead us is to restore to us the belief in our own guidance."

In practical, business terms, "empowering" others means that today's leaders like to delegate, to urge others to share the vision
and get involved. . . . Even more important, you raise the individual level of aspiration; you strengthen self-confidence. That's
what Napoleon was talking about when he observed that "a leader
is a dealer in hope."
                              —Lloyd E. Reuss

If you pick the right people and give them the opportunity to spread
their wings—and put compensation as a carrier behind it—you
almost don't have to manage them.
                              —Jack Welch

(*See* Control, Delegating Authority, People-Centering,
                              Teamwork.)

Encouragement

There is not one of you who has not in his knapsack the field
marshal's baton; it is up to you to bring it out.
                              —Louis XVIII
                              Speech to the Saint-Cyr cadets, 1819

Old praise dies, unless you feed it.
                              —English proverb

Let us therefore animate and encourage each other, and show the whole world, that a Freeman contending for *Liberty* on his own ground is superior to any slavish mercenary on earth.
—General George Washington
General Order to the Continental
Army, July 2, 1776

(*See* Incentive, Motivation, People-Centering, Praise.)

Enemies

The need for social esteem . . . is a powerful one . . . almost all leaders, at least on the national level, must settle for far less than universal affection. They must be willing *to make enemies*—to deny themselves the affection of their adversaries. They must accept conflict. They must be willing and able to be unloved. It is hard to pick one's friends, harder to pick one's enemies.
—James MacGregor Burns

Hug your friends tight, but your enemies tighter—hug 'em so tight they can't wiggle.
—Old Texas maxim

(*See* Opponents.)

Enthusiasm

Preserve your enthusiasm for playing. Loss of that enthusiasm is deadly to musicianship.
—Artur Rubinstein

Know how to put fire into your subordinates.
—Baltasar Gracián

Entrepreneurial Spirit

We are very short on people who know how to do anything. So please don't set out to make money. Set out to make something and hope you get rich in the process.
> —Andy Rooney
> Commencement address

Love what you're doing.
Believe in your product.
Select good people.
> —Debbi Fields

I've told you that success is not easily won. It requires sacrifice and hard work. Even with these, you risk the pain of failure. Don't let that put you off. The Risk-Reward Ratio is on your side. I think the return on this investment is best described in Hooker's translation of *Cyrano de Bergerac*. In it, the Compte de Guiche, with reference to Don Quixote, reminds Cyrano that "windmills, if you fight them, may swing around their huge arms and cast you down into the mire." A defiant Cyrano, speaking for all entrepreneurs, replies, "Or up among the stars."
> —Victor Kiam

(*See* Profit and Loss, Starting a Business, Venturing.)

Ethics in Business

Never undertake anything unless you have the heart to ask Heaven's blessing on your undertaking.
> —Georg Christoph Lichtenberg

Subordinates cannot be left to speculate as to the values of the organization. Top leadership must give forth clear and explicit signals, lest any confusion or uncertainty exist over what is and is not permissible conduct. To do otherwise allows informal and potentially subversive "codes of conduct" to be transmitted with a wink and a nod, and encourages an inferior ethical system based on "going along to get along" or on the notion that "everybody's doing it."

—Richard Thornburgh

Never let a man imagine that he can pursue a good end by evil means, without sinning against his own soul. The evil effect on himself is certain.

—Robert Southey

If we believe a thing to be bad, and if we have a right to prevent it, it is our duty to try to prevent it and damn the consequences.

—Lord Milner

Let no pleasure tempt thee, no profit allure thee, no persuasion move thee, to do anything which thou knowest to be evil; so shalt thou always live jollily; for a good conscience is a continual Christmas.

—Benjamin Franklin

If you stand straight, do not fear a crooked shadow.

—Chinese proverb

Do not steal a loaf from the man who kneads and bakes it.

—Cervantes

Except in poker, bridge, and similar play-period activities, *don't con anybody. Don't con yourself either.*

—Robert Townsend

Be not allured, my friend, by cunning gains.

—Pindar

Basic precepts of business ethics:
1. Stay within the purview of the law—follow the general spirit of the law. (Ignorance of the law is no excuse, but today no one can be well informed as to all the laws and their

application to business. So see your counsel if it is indicated.)
2. If you can't talk about it openly, don't do it. If it would make
   you uncomfortable to read it on the front page of *The New
   York Times*, don't do it.
3. If you cannot book the transaction exactly the way it occurred,
   don't do it.

—William H. Frey and A. Worth
Loomis

Be above the little arts and tricks of small men, and if you grow
rich, let it be by honest and patient industry. Build not up a fortune
from the labors of others, from the unpaid debts of creditors, from
the uncertain games of chance, but from manly effort which never
goes unrewarded. Never engage in any business unless you can be
honest in it; if it will not give a fair living without fraud, leave it,
as you would the gate of death.

—Daniel C. Eddy

Be sure your sin will find you out.

—Numbers 32:23

Make money. Have fun. Be ethical. These are the three keys to a
successful business career, given to me years ago by my boss. I've
repeated them to everybody I've ever hired. Sometimes an eye-
brow will go up. Ethics? Some people don't think of that as a
necessary part of a first-day briefing. It's not in their frame of
reference. And that's exactly what the problem is.

—Don Peppers

There's only one standard. Once you're stuck on the flypaper,
you're stuck. If you don't set a high standard you can't expect your
people to act right.

—Donald M. Kendall

(*See* Honesty.)

Evaluation

Look for the good things, not the faults. It takes a good deal bigger-sized brain to find out what is not wrong with people and things, than to find out what is wrong.
—R. L. Sharpe

Will you tell me, Master Shallow, how to choose a man? Care I for the limb, the thews, the stature, bulk and big assemblance of a man? Give me the spirit, Master Shallow.
—Falstaff, in Shakespeare's 2 *Henry IV*

Look at the means which a man employs, consider his motives, observe his pleasures. A man simply cannot conceal himself!
—Confucius

Using the wisdom of strategy, think of the enemy as your own troops. When you think in this way, you can move him at will and be able to chase him around. You become the general and the enemy becomes your troops.
—Miyamoto Musashi

When you're off on a business trip or vacation, pretend you're a customer. Telephone some part of your organization and ask for help. You'll run into some real horror shows. . . . Try calling yourself up, and see what indignities you've built into your own defenses.
—Robert Townsend

Never esteem men on account of their riches or their station. Respect goodness, find it where you may.
—William Cobbett
Advice to Young Men

Get to know two things about a man—how he earns his money and how he spends it—and you have the clue to his character, for you have a searchlight that shows up the innermost recesses of his soul. You know all you need to know about his standards, his motives, his driving desires, and his real religion.
—Robert J. McCracken

Look beyond appearances. Things are not always as they seem. . . . An American diplomat was rumored to be a heavy drinker—a rumor based, in part, on an occurrence at a diplomatic function at a U.S. embassy in South America.

When the orchestra struck up, the diplomat felt that—as the senior American official present—he should start the dancing. Spying a gorgeously robed figure, he said: "Beautiful lady in scarlet, will you do me the honor of waltzing with me?"

"Certainly not," came the sharp response. "In the first place, you are drunk. In the second, this is not a waltz but the Venezuelan national anthem, and thirdly, I am not a beautiful lady in scarlet; I am, in fact, the papal nuncio."
—Robert L. Clark

I have known a vast quantity of nonsense talked about bad men not looking you in the face. Don't trust that conventional idea. Dishonesty will stare honesty out of countenance any day in the week if there is anything to be got by it.
—Charles Dickens

To succeed in the world, it is much more necessary to possess the penetration to discern who is a fool, than to discover who is a clever man.
—Talleyrand

(*See* Capabilities, Character, Contacts, Firing, Hiring, Proficiency.)

Example

You have to set the tone and pace, define objectives and strategies, demonstrate through personal example what you expect from others.
—Stanley C. Gault

Be a pattern to others, and then all will go well: for as a whole city is affected by the licentious passions of great men, so it is likewise reformed by their moderation.

—Cicero

Neither shall you allege the example of the many as an excuse for doing wrong.

—Exodus 23:2

(*See* Bosses, Leadership [Personal], Standards.)

Excellence

Demand the best from yourself, because others will demand the best of you. . . . Successful people don't simply give a project hard work. They give it their best work.

—Win Borden

Whatever you do, you should want to be the best at it. Every time you approach a task, you should be aiming to do the best job that's ever been done at it and not stop until you've done it. Anyone who does that will be successful—and rich.

—David Ogilvy

Your adrenaline has to run. Whatever business you are in, if you don't feel exhilarated by achieving your objectives and excelling in what you're doing, then you will never do very much well. You can do a lot of things competently. But you have to have a sense of being turned on by the thought of making something go well. It's doing something better than it has ever been done before, or creating a new refinement in what you're making or a better service than the other guy. This is how you build a business.

—Malcolm Forbes

Always remember what you're good at and stick with it.

—Ermenegildo Zegna

(*See* Capabilities, People-Centering, Productivity, Proficiency, Standards.)

Executive Health

Always do one thing less than you think you can do.
            —Bernard M. Baruch

Improve your health and your appearance; get away from stresses . . . spas are becoming an increasingly important part of American life. The 7-day miracle, as some refer to a week's spa vacation, provides you with a necessary interlude to change your pace of life and your way of being, to lose weight, shape up, reduce stress, gain confidence, reassess your goals, recharge your vitality, learn new exercise and nutrition behaviors, reward yourself with time out for yourself—and have a good time, a carefree holiday. ("For arm toning, you may try to keep a rubber ball submerged in the pool. Hard to do!")
            —Theodore B. Van Itallie, M.D., and
            Leila Hadley

When you have a lot of things to do, get your nap out of the way first.
            —Jeremiah Hines (from his daughter Jo
            Anderson), quoted by Paul Dickson

Never get sick, Hubert; there isn't time.
            —Hubert H. Humphrey's father

(*See* Family Values, Fun, Recreation, Stress, Workaholism.)

Executive Women

Don't take shortcuts. Take as much responsibility as, and more than, you think you can handle.

Work twice as hard and three times as long as a man in the same position. Keep going; you win out in the end, even though you might not think so.

Don't sit back and be the smiley one. Be aggressive but not repulsive. Let them know you're there or they'll never see you.
>   —*Wall Street Journal*

Don't try to be one of the boys. Be yourself. Capitalize on your female strengths and use the psychological tools you have acquired to deal with male chauvinism as well as to climb the ladder of success.
>   —Dr. Joyce Brothers

You are going to be judged by the company you keep. Seek out the people who can help you. Men have known this for years, and we are playing in their arena.
>   —Anne P. Hyde

If you want to succeed, you'd better look as if you mean business.
>   —Jeanne Holm

Expediency

Ask yourself not if this or that is expedient, but if it is right.
>   —Alan Paton

Where principle is involved, be deaf to expediency.
                    —Matthew Fontaine Maury, Navy
                    oceanographer

(*See* Principles.)

Experience

Never buy a saddle until you have met the horse.
                    —Mortimer B. Zuckerman

What man would be wise, let him drink of the river
That bears on its bosom the record of time;
A message to him every wave can deliver
To teach him to creep till he knows how to climb.
                    —John Boyle O'Reilly

Draw from other people's dangers the lesson that may profit yourself.
                    —Terence

Experimentation

One thing is sure. We have to do something. We have to do the best we know how at the moment. . . . If it doesn't turn out right, we can modify it as we go along.
                    —Franklin D. Roosevelt, counseling
                    Frances Perkins

"Do it, fix it, try it," is our favorite axiom. Karl Weick adds that "chaotic action is preferable to orderly inaction." . . . The most important and visible outcropping of the action bias in the excellent

companies is their willingness to try things out, to experiment.
—Thomas J. Peters and Robert H.
Waterman, Jr.

One must look for one thing only, to find many.
—Cesare Pavese

If you wish to advance into the infinite, explore the finite in all directions.
—Goethe

Let your imagination go, guiding it by judgment and principle, but holding it in and directing it by *experiment*.
—Michael Faraday

Put off your imagination, as you put off your overcoat, when you enter a laboratory. But put it on again, as you put on your overcoat, when you leave.
—Charles Bernard

How do I work? I grope.
—Albert Einstein

(*See* New Ideas, Research and Development.)

Experts

We must all consult doctors, lawyers, bankers and other specialists to help us, but view experts with a jaundiced eye. Trust your own knowledge and instincts. When something sounds fishy, ask, "Says who? Where is it written?" Is the expert there to help you—or to attend to a bigger client, to please the boss, to get personal visibility or to win a better job? Never assume that so-called professionalism will protect you.
—David Mahoney

Experts should be on tap but never on top.
—Winston Churchill

F

Failing

Keep in mind that neither success nor failure is ever final.
—Roger Babson

Screw your courage to the sticking-place
And we'll not fail.
—Lady Macbeth, in Shakespeare's
Macbeth

Meet your failure nobly, and it will not differ from success.
—Ralph Waldo Emerson

Teach a highly educated person that it is not a disgrace to fail and that he must analyze every failure to find its cause. He must learn how to fail intelligently, for failing is one of the greatest arts in the world.
—Charles F. Kettering

The surest way not to fail is to determine to succeed.
—Richard Brinsley Sheridan

It's necessary not to fear the prospect of failure but to be determined not to fail.
—Jimmy Carter

Test fast, fail fast, adjust fast.
—Tom Peters

If you're worried about that last at bat, you're going to be miserable, you're only going to get depressed, but if you put a picture in your mind that you're going to get a base hit off him the next time, now how do you feel? I try to put positive pictures into the minds of my players.
—Tommy Lasorda

The best way not to fail again is to be absolutely positive that when you do it this time, you're going to do it right.
—Burt Reynolds

Family Values

O friends, be men; so act that none may feel
Ashamed to meet the eyes of other men.
Think each one of his children and his wife,
His home, his parents, living yet or dead.
For them, the absent ones, I supplicate,
And bid you rally here, and scorn to fly.
—Homer

The most important thing to remember is that you can't give *all* of yourself to anything. . . . The only way you stay detached enough to face up to the pressures and deal in a controlled and positive manner with the source of your worries is to make sure you have a life away from your work, and for me that has always been my family.
— Roy Ash

Get yourself a spouse. Some things you just can't blame on the media or the government.
—David Mahoney

(*See* Fun, Recreation.)

Favorites

Never play favorites. Make your men feel that justice tempered with mercy may always be counted on. This does not mean a slackening of discipline. Obedience to orders and regulations must always be insisted upon, and good conduct on the part of the men exacted.

—John A. Lejeune
Letter to officers, U.S. Marine Corps, 1920

Let appointments and removals be made on business principles, and by fixed rules. . . . Let no man be put . . . out or in merely because he is our friend.

—Rutherford B. Hayes

(*See* Nepotism.)

Fear

The time to take counsel of your fears is before you make an important battle decision. That's the time to listen to every fear you can imagine! When you have collected all the facts and fears and made your decision, turn off all of your fears and go ahead!

—General George S. Patton, Jr.

Consider that it is useful to engender fear, or at least a high degree of anxiety: . . . Your operation faces a critical deadline. Your management style has been participatory. Your key people are used to deliberating. . . . You correctly demand: "Don't talk about it. Just DO it, or else!" . . . Use a jolt of fear. . . . Make the fear situational, not personal—emphasize that the employee should be afraid of the consequences of his own actions, not of you as a person. . . . It's bad to keep subordinates in a miasma of chronic fear.

But concentrated doses of pinpointed fear—when accompanied by the means of overcoming the fear—can be a useful management tool. Authority means power, and power can inspire fear. When necessary, use it. Otherwise, you'll lose it.
                                —Mortimer R. Feinberg

(*See* Obedience.)

Firing and Being Fired

Severities should be dealt out all at once, that by their suddenness they may give less offense; benefits should be handed out drop by drop, that they be relished the more.
                                —Niccolò Machiavelli

If your managers prove to be incompetent, or let you down, get rid of them. This is often the hardest part of a top executive job, unless you are sadistically inclined, for there is no kind way to kick somebody downstairs. To minimize the pain, be straightforward (no double talk), spare the victim's ego (no scorn, no anger) and make it fast (no twisting in the wind).
                                —William Attwood

What is best for the enterprise must govern the person with chief responsibility. As he should not appoint on old friendship alone, he must at times remove an old friend, though it be always painful and sometimes even unfair.
                                —Vermont Royster

        . . . Think him as a serpent's egg
    Which hatch'd would as his kind grow mischievous,
    And kill him in the shell.
                                —Brutus, in Shakespeare's *Julius Caesar*

Do be careful that you don't throw the baby out with the bathwater, and find yourself with too many people who lack experience.
                                —J. P. Young

Care should be taken that the punishment does not exceed the guilt; and also that some men do not suffer for offenses for which others are not even indicted.
                                                                —Cicero

On being fired:
Keep in mind that you would not have gotten so far in your career without having considerable ability. . . . Approach being fired with the same kind of strength you have given to the job. That means letting the guy who's firing you know you're not happy about it.
                                                —Dr. Robert T. London

Resist the impulse to get on the phone immediately to tell all your friends and business contacts that you're being let go and "do you know of anything?" Putting them on the spot can be embarrassing, and if someone is aware of an opening elsewhere, you should be properly prepared to pursue the lead. And—unless you've been in the habit of changing jobs often—it will take time to draw up a proper résumé, get a fix on your salary requirements and future goals, and otherwise prepare yourself. Recognize that you may be in for a long search. Apply at once for unemployment benefits, and put the family on an austerity program. Don't waste time by taking a vacation before starting the hunt.
                                                —*Business Week*

If you have been fired, the first thing is to forget about killing yourself. . . . The second thing is to get another job . . . swallow your pride and immediately contact everyone you ever knew who might be helpful. Then be honest in the interviews they steer you to. If you were fired, say so . . . tell them why you think you were kicked out. Don't grouse, just explain. . . . But don't accuse the person who kicked you out of being an s.o.b. Nobody wants to hire a sniveler. . . . It's important, as you search for work, to stick with the thing you know. . . . Be eager to relocate. . . . Most of all, don't give up. Keep trying. Stay motivated, no matter what. Remember that many of us have gone through the hell you are going through.
                                                —Tim H. Henney

(*See* Evaluation.)

Focus

Here is the prime condition of success: Concentrate your energy, thought and capital exclusively upon the business in which you are engaged. Having begun on one line, resolve to fight it out on that line, to lead in it, adopt every improvement, have the best machinery, and know the most about it.
—Andrew Carnegie

Keep focused on the substantive issues. To make a decision means having to go through one door and closing all others.
— Abraham Zaleznik

Forecasting

When you hurt your left ankle, watch out for your right knee.
—David Mahoney

If you can't forecast accurately, forecast often.
—Proverb for economists quoted by
Leonard Silk

Always ask an economist what will happen if his forecast is wrong. . . . Never believe an economist who tells you to abandon your common sense.
—Alice Rivlin

Fortunetellers, chart readers, and any others who program people subconsciously or consciously with negative self-fulfilling prophecies are dangerous people. Never allow these people to move into the control position of your life.
—Robert H. Schuller

He who lives by the crystal ball will end up eating ground glass.
—Anon.

(*See* Gut Feelings, Hunches, Planning, Strategic Planning.)

Frustration

Frustration is your worst enemy. You have to continue to stop
yourself from letting frustration drive you to make irrational decisions—or rely on your advisers to stop you. When we put a deal
together, I have the ability to focus on exactly what we're working
on and close everything else out.
—Henry R. Kravis

(*See* Patience.)

Fun

Take the world as you find it; enjoy everything. "Viva la bagatelle!"
—Benjamin Disraeli

Have fun. I don't kid myself. Life is very fragile, and success doesn't
change that. If anything, success makes it more fragile. Anything
can change, without warning, and that's why I try not to take any
of what's happened too seriously.
—Donald J. Trump

Play so that you may be serious.
—Anacharsis (c. 600 B.C.)

(*See* Family Values, Recreation.)

The Future

In *A Woman of the Future*, Australian novelist David Freland
described a character whose "past was before him like a beacon;
he would keep going in that direction and call it the future." To
be in control, to master change, to be a supermanager in a time
of rapid, turbulent, and confusing change, you must fall away from
a past that prevents you from seeing the potential ahead.
                              —Arnold Brown and Edith Weiner

G

Generalists

Tomorrow's leaders will very likely have begun life as trained specialists, but to mature as leaders they must sooner or later climb out of the trenches of specialization and rise above the boundaries that separate the various segments of society. Only as generalists can they cope with the diversity of problems and multiple constituencies that contemporary leaders face.
                                    —John W. Gardner

Genius

Beware the genius manager. Management is doing a very few simple things and doing them well. You put brilliant people into staff roles. But for crissakes don't let them ever make decisions, because the secret of management is never to make a decision which ordinary human beings can't carry out. . . . Most of the time it is hard work to get a very few simple things across so that ordinary people can do it.
                                    —Peter F. Drucker

Talk not of genius baffled. Genius is master of
   man.
Genius does what it must, and talent does what
   it can.
                              —Owen Meredith

Get Up and Go

If you don't make dust, you eat dust.
                    —Motto of Jack A. MacAllister

Do not lie in a ditch, and say God help me; use the lawful tools
He hath lent thee.
                              —English proverb

(*See* Action, Implementation.)

Gifts (Corporate)

If the gift is for a business associate, it is usually more suitable to
send it to the recipient's home than to his or her office. That way,
others in the office can't make mental notes about who sent whom
what.
   The note that accompanies the gift is as important as the gift
itself. . . . A present should be accompanied by a hand-written
card. The message can be as short as: "To Bob and his family: I
hope your Christmas will be great, and your [next year] terrific!"
Or, in a more sober key, "To Bob, with my very best wishes for
a wonderful holiday season. We appreciate the fine work you have
done for us this year." It doesn't matter what you say: what matters
is that you wrote it yourself.
                              —Letitia Baldrige

While you look at what is given, look also at the giver.
                    —Seneca

                  (*See* Kindliness, Travel.)

Globalization

The root cause of change in the nineties will be globalization. You'll
have to have global standards for quality, for pricing, for service,
for design. You will have to have global leadership.
                    —Noel Tichy

No one's going to be able to operate without a grounding in the
basic sciences. Language would be helpful, although English is
becoming increasingly international. And travel. You have to have
a global attitude.
                    —Rupert Murdoch

Hands-on international experience is moving out of the "nice but
not necessary" category and into the "must have" slot for those on
the corporate fast track. [Four rules to follow:]
    —Beef up the skills level in international divisions.
    —Help managers shake off the assumption that products or
      methods that work at home will automatically work in foreign
      lands.
    —Gain insights into how foreign competitors operate and form
      strategy.
    —Give those on the fast track experience in running a good-
      sized operation without constant oversight from headquarters.
                    —Claudia H. Deutsch

While company managements can—and in my opinion should—
carry out ethical policies abroad, they must do so with due regard
for local practice and sensitivities, in a flexible manner that takes
account of local law and builds consent among their local partners,

boards and employees rather than by exercise of a corporate sledge-
hammer.
                          —Stanley Cleveland

Goading

Stephen Jobs turned to an early Apple consultant, mechanical en-
gineer David M. Kelley, to implement Esslinger's design. At first,
Kelley worried that Jobs' demands—for instance, a tilt mechanism
for the monitor—would be too difficult to pull off. "You want to
be the voice of reason," says Kelley. "But when I would say: 'Steve,
that's going to be too expensive,' or, 'It can't be done,' his response
was: 'You wimp.' He makes you feel like a small thinker." So Kelley
and a team of six engineers worked around the clock to turn Esslinger's design into a mechanical reality.
                          —*Business Week* story by Katherine
                          Hafner and Richard Brandt

If you really want to get a line group motivated, just float up a
"staff idea" with the right amount of "Why didn't you guys think
of this?"
                          —Lee J. Iacocca

        (*See* Motivation.)

Goals

If you don't know where you are going, you will probably wind up
somewhere else.
                          —Dr. Laurence J. Peter

Goals must be under your control. We need targets and directions
upon which to focus our efforts. "Winning" is one such target;

however, it is an impractical one. Winning is not totally under our control. . . . Instead of setting goals based on outcomes, we should set goals which focus on our performance, such as hitting 80 percent of our drives on the fairway. By setting goals which we control, we will not be as influenced by such factors as the opponent, the weather, the problems we may be having at home or on the job, or even luck. . . . Breaking down goals into small manageable steps is essential. As an African proverb states: "The best way to eat the elephant standing in your path is to cut it up into little pieces."
—Steven J. Danish

I work on the same principle as people who train horses. You start with low fences, easily achieved goals, and work up. It's important in management never to ask people to try to accomplish goals they can't accept.
—Ian MacGregor

You must have long-range goals to keep you from being frustrated by short-range failures.
—Charles C. Noble

As you go through life, brother
Whatever be your goal.
Keep your eye upon the doughnut
And not upon the hole.
—Mayflower Coffee Shop slogan

Set positive goals and reasonable expectations.
—Steve Strasser

(See Higher Purpose, Inspiration, Vision.)

Governing

In all that the people can individually do as well for themselves, government ought not to interfere.
—Abraham Lincoln

There are only three rules of sound administration: pick good men, tell them not to cut corners, and back them to the limit; and picking good men is the most important.
—Adlai E. Stevenson

Graciousness

Whenever you write to persons greatly your inferiors, and by way of giving orders, let your letters speak, what I hope to God you will always feel, the utmost gentleness and humanity. If you happen to write to your *valet de chambre* or your bailiff, it is no great trouble to say, *Pray, do such a thing;* it will be taken kindly, and your orders will be the better executed for it.
—Lord Chesterfield

Gratitude

Don't drown the man who taught you to swim. If you learned your trade or profession of the man, do not set up in opposition to him. Do not kick down the ladder by which you climbed. *Yet this unnatural course of action seems natural to some, as we know right well.*
—C. H. Spurgeon

Greasy Pole

There is only so much that any one Patron can do for you. To draw an analogy, an experienced mountaineer can pull a weaker climber up to his level. Then the leader must himself climb higher before he can exert more pull.

But if the first Patron *cannot climb higher*, then the Pullee must find another Patron who can.

So be prepared, when the time comes, to switch your allegiance to another Patron of higher rank than the first.

"There's no Patron like a new Patron!"

> —Dr. Laurence J. Peter and Raymond Hull

I had made myself almost too good as Number Two. So, in effect, what I had to do to get promoted was to get my boss promoted. Which I would advise anyone. That may sound cynical, but if you want to get ahead, promote your boss.

> —William George

If you can't bear to have your face stepped on, don't try to climb the ladder of success.

> —Evan Esar

Greatness

Brains every day become more precious than blood. You must give men new ideas, you must teach them new words, you must modify their manners, you must change their laws, you must root out prejudices, subvert convictions, if you wish to be great.

Beware of endeavoring to become a great man in a hurry. One such attempt in ten thousand may succeed. These are fearful odds.

> —Benjamin Disraeli

(*See* Heroism.)

Greed

Grasp no more than thy hand will hold.
                    —English proverb

(*See* Insider Trading.)

Growth

If you want to be a big company tomorrow, start acting like one
today.
                    —Peter F. Drucker

You've got to do things differently when you get to a certain size
or you're going to suffer.
                    —H. Brewster Atwater, Jr.

Gut Feelings

To be successful in using power you have to have a sense of power.
I would define that as a gut-feel of being able to predict with some
degree of certainty how people will react in certain situations, so
you can predict when there is going to be trouble over something.
                    —W. Michael Blumenthal

Trust your gut.

                    — Barbara Walters

[Freud once advised:] "Anything that's important, don't think
about. Do what you feel like doing. When I think back on my own

decisions, the truly satisfying ones often 'felt right' before I made them." Freud was really saying "trust yourself"—a piece of advice so wise that it has existed in various forms for thousands of years.
> —Dr. Harold Greenwald with Elizabeth Rich

Never ignore a gut feeling, but never believe that it's enough.
> —Robert Heller

We should only believe in our feelings, after the soul has been long at rest from them; and express ourselves, not as we feel but as we remember.
> —Joseph Joubert

Let him make use of instinct who cannot make use of reason.
> —John Ray proverb

Never use intuition.
> —General Omar N. Bradley

(*See* Forecasting, Hunches, Intelligence, Strategic Planning.)

H

Hands-On Managing

If you want some ham, you gotta go into the smokehouse.
—Huey Long, quoted by Lane Kirkland

When you get right down to it, one of the most important tasks of a manager is to eliminate his people's excuses for failure. But if you're a paper manager, hiding in your office, they may not tell you about the problems only you can solve. So get out and ask them if there's anything you can do to help. Pretty soon they're standing right out there in the open with nobody but themselves to blame. Then they get to work, then they turn on to success, and then they have the strength of ten.
—Robert Townsend

He who would eat the fruit must climb the tree.
—Scottish proverb

If officers desire to have control over their commands, they must remain habitually with them, industriously attend to their instruction and comfort, and in battle lead them well.
—General Thomas J. "Stonewall" Jackson

The accumulation of little items, each too "trivial" to trouble the boss with, is the prime cause of miss-the-market delays. As boss,

105

you must consciously seek out opportunities to help in little ways. You must view yourself as basher-in-chief of small barriers and facilitator-in-chief of trivial aids to action rather than "the great planner."

—Tom Peters

(*See* High Tech, Visible Management.)

Hard Work

I think I had a flair for [politics] but natural feelings are never enough. You've got to marry those natural feelings with really hard work—but the hard work comes more easily when you are doing things that you want to do.

—Margaret Thatcher

Let me . . . remind you that it is only by working with an energy which is almost superhuman and which looks to uninterested spectators like insanity that we can accomplish anything worth the achievement. Work is the keystone of a perfect life. Work and trust in God.

—Woodrow Wilson

Do not expect the success that comes from easy accomplishment and ready recognition. What will justify the effort if all there is before you is defeat and renewed struggle? You must not learn to expect success in order to justify your efforts. You must learn to need only to *think* the effort necessary, whatever the outcome. Great things are not accomplished by the shouters but by the workers. But to learn to work—that is a hard task indeed.

—Jacob Neusner

I always told my managers that you can't be successful unless you tell your wife not to expect you home for dinner.

—C. Kemmons Wilson, founder of
Holiday Inns

Like any other compulsive behavior, as important as the long and hard hours will be for your success, you will one day have to learn to moderate at least the extreme edge of your excess. No one can work forever without paying the price. "We all leak oil." The quote . . . is Lee Trevino's, meant, of course, to point out that even a pro has a heart and a nervous system.
—Thomas F. Jones

(*See* Dedication, Executive Health, Recreation, Workaholism.)

Headhunters

One attracts the attention of headhunters the same way one attracts the attention of potential employers or, for that matter, one's boss's boss—by making oneself visible. . . . The research departments of search firms read and clip financial and trade papers. Do something to get yourself mentioned, and you will end up in the major headhunters' files. If your extracurricular activities include work in charitable, political, or civic organizations, as they should, you are going to meet search people somewhere along the line. . . . Search people are good people to make friends with.
—Lester Korn

Headquarters Staff

When a favourite grows insolent, it is wisdom to raise another into favour, who may give check to the other's presumption.
—Thomas Fuller

The first-rate man will try to surround himself with his equals, or better if possible. The second-rate man will surround himself with

third-rate men. The third-rate man will surround himself with fifth-rate men.
—André Weil

Be as careful as you can to look objectively at what you do as to how it might be construed from an appearance standpoint.
—Charles Wick

The leading qualifications which should distinguish an officer for the head of staff are, to know the country thoroughly; to be able to conduct a reconnaissance with skill; to superintend the transmission of orders promptly; to lay down the most complicated movements intelligibly, but in a few words with simplicity.
—Napoleon I

Have a deputy and use him. Don't be consumed by the job or you will lose your balance. . . . Balance is critically important to your performance.
—Donald H. Rumsfeld

(*See* Advisers, Evaluation.)

Heroism

A democracy cannot follow a leader unless he is dramatized. A man to be a hero must not content himself with heroic virtues and anonymous action. He must talk and explain as he acts—drama.
—William Allen White

Nurture your mind with great thoughts. To believe in the heroic makes heroes.
— Benjamin Disraeli

The characteristic of a genuine heroism is its persistency. All men have wandering impulses, fits and starts of generosity. But when you have resolved to be great, abide by yourself, and do not weakly try to reconcile yourself with the world. The heroic cannot be the common, nor the common the heroic.

—Ralph Waldo Emerson

(*See* Greatness.)

Hierarchy

Let all your things have their places; let each part of your business have its time.

—Benjamin Franklin

Put things in their places, and they will put you in your place.

—Arabic proverb

(*See* Organization.)

Higher Purpose

I hold that while man exists it is his duty to improve not only his own condition, but to assist in ameliorating mankind; and, therefore, without entering upon the details of the question, I will simply say that I am for those means which will give the greatest good to the greatest number.

—Abraham Lincoln

Develop a train of thought on which to ride. The nobility of your life as well as your happiness depends upon the direction in which that chain of thought is going.

—Dr. Laurence J. Peter

Running a business is not the important thing but making a commitment to do the whole job, making a commitment to improve things, to influence the world is. One of the most satisfying things is to help others to be creative, to take responsibility, to be challenged in their jobs.

—Kenneth H. Olsen

(*See* Corporate Giving, Long View, Philanthropy, Public Service, Vision.)

High Tech

Without question we need technology. But we must find ways to add back the human touch it subtracts. . . . There are always forces of evil interfering with the natural order of the universe. In our time they are the alienation, repression and conformity of the technological age. We must fight them, but we must also look beyond them and see the possibilities technology opens to us to enhance individuality.

—Allan H. Clark

Remember, behind the glamorous headlines and stories on technology are always human drive and energy—human cause and effect. . . . What I'm urging here is that we not lose sight of the human side of what is happening around us. . . . Yes, technology is of growing importance. But let's keep it in perspective and view it as a tool, not some element taking on a life of its own.

—John D. Nichols

Look at those cows and remember that the greatest scientists in the world have never discovered how to make grass into milk.

—Michael Pupin

Understand the technology you work for so well that you control *it* instead of letting *it* control *you*.

—George W. Dudley

(*See* Hands-On Managing.)

Hiring

Hire people who are better than you are, then leave them to get on with it. . . . Look for people who will aim for the remarkable, who will not settle for the routine.
                    —David Ogilvy

Do not put the saddle on the wrong horse.
                    —English proverb

If thou has a regard for thrift, keep no more cats than will kill mice.
                    —J. Dare, 1673

When you can't afford to hire the best, hire the young who are going to be the best.
                    —Geraldine Stutz

Let him sing to the flute who cannot sing to the harp.
                    —Cicero

(*See* Evaluation.)

Homework

My rule always was to do the business of the day in the day.
                    —Arthur Wellesley, Duke of Wellington

Honesty

We need to stress that personal integrity is as important as executive skill in business dealings. . . . Setting an example from the

top has a ripple effect throughout a business school or a corporation. After nearly three decades in business, 10 years as chief executive of a Big Eight accounting firm, I have learned that the standards set at the top filter throughout a company. . . . [Quoting Professor Thomas Dunfee of the Wharton School:] "A company that fails to take steps to produce a climate conducive to positive work-related ethical attitudes may create a vacuum in which employees so predisposed may foster a frontier-style, everyone for themselves mentality."
                                          —Russell E. Palmer

Don't measure your neighbor's honesty by your own.
                                          —American proverb

Be a terror to the butchers, that they may be fair in their weight; and keep hucksters and fraudulent dealers in awe, for the same reason.
                                          —Cervantes

(*See* Ethics in Business, Shading the Truth, Standards, Truth in Advertising.)

Hubris

Use your prosperity with so much caution and prudence as may not suffer you to forget yourself, or despise your inferior.
                                          —George Shelley

Stand to your work and be wise, certain of sword and pen,
Being neither children, nor gods, but men in a world of men.
                                          —Rudyard Kipling

Talk not of your personal success to one who has failed; forget not your failures in your moment of success.
>
> —Mr. Tut-Tut (17th cent.)
> Translated by Lin Yutang

(*See* Attitude, Ego Trips, Humility, Power.)

Humility

A man ought always to be a little more humble than his rank would require, not accepting too readily the favors and honors that are offered him, but modestly refusing them while showing that he esteems them highly, yet in such a way as to give the donor cause to press them upon him more urgently. For the greater the resistance shown by accepting them in this way, the more will the prince who is granting them think himself to be esteemed.
>
> —Baldassare Castiglione
> *The Book of the Courtier,* 1528

Always acknowledge a fault frankly. This will throw those in authority off their guard and give you opportunity to commit more.
>
> —Mark Twain

Show no scorn of inferiors.
>
> —Claudian

Never forget the hard times and the early days. Always remember where you came from.
>
> —David Liederman

(*See* Ego Trips, Hubris, Perspective.)

Humor

Use your wit as a shield, not as a dagger.
                    —American proverb

. . . a sense of humor can be a great help—particularly a sense of humor about [oneself]. William Howard Taft joked about his own corpulence and people loved it; it took nothing from his inherent dignity. Lincoln eased tense moments with bawdy stories, and often poked fun at himself—and history honors him for this human quality. A sense of humor is part of the art of leadership, of getting along with people, of getting things done.
                    —Dwight D. Eisenhower

Be amusing; never tell unkind stories; above all, never tell long ones.
                    —Benjamin Disraeli

Women should not only have a sense of humor but the ability to use it appropriately and sometimes irreverently in business dealings. If one doesn't take oneself too seriously, it tends to have men accept you more quickly. I would say that this is a distinguishing characteristic in successful women.
                    —Jane Evans

Hunches

The chief executive officer is not supposed to say, "I feel." He's supposed to say "I know." . . . So we deify the word "instinct" by calling it "judgment." . . . Follow your [hunches] like the ancient navigators followed the stars. The voyage may be lonely, but the stars will take you where you want to go.
                    —David Mahoney

Don't tune out your hunch. . . . It's easy to intellectualize or analyze your way out of heeding a hunch. The trouble is you *know*, but you don't know how you know. So remind yourself that this feeling, this little whisper from deep inside your brain, may contain far more information—both facts and impressions—than you're likely to obtain from hours of analysis.
　　　　　　　　　—Roy Rowan

You can't solve many of today's problems by straight linear thinking. It takes leaps of faith to sense the connections that are not necessarily obvious.
　　　　　　　　　—Matina Horner

Always try to feel the emotion you ought to feel.
　　　　　　　　　—William Churchill King

(*See* Forecasting, Gut Feelings, Intelligence, Strategic Planning.)

I

Identity

Do not free a camel of the burden of his hump; you may be freeing him from being a camel.
—Gilbert Keith Chesterton

If you don't know what business you are in, conceptualize what business it would be useful for you to think you are in.
—John Naisbitt

Image

Abstain from all appearance of evil.
—St. Paul
First Epistle to the Thessalonians

It is not essential . . . that a prince should have all the good qualities. . . . But it is most essential that he should seem to have them.
—Niccolò Machiavelli

116

The smile, as most any tactic, has its risks. It must not appear foolish or project ridicule; nor should it look like an arrogant smirk.
—Myles Martel (who helped coach
Ronald Reagan in his 1980 debates)

You can't lead a cavalry charge if you think you look funny on a horse.
—John Peers

Nobody should look anxious except those who have no anxiety.

Whenever you see a man who is successful in society, try to discover what makes him pleasing, and if possible adopt his system.
—Benjamin Disraeli

Assume a virtue, if you have it not.
—Hamlet, in Shakespeare's *Hamlet*

(*See* Attitude, Ego Trips, Hubris, Humility, Power.)

Impetuousness

Beware of mettle in a blind horse. He is apt to dash into danger. He must go, and he does not see where. Many zealots are so ignorant that they come under this proverb; they are dangerous when they are not well-guided.
—C. H. Spurgeon

Implementation

Let us diligently apply the means, never doubting that a just God, in His own good time, will give us the rightful result.
—Abraham Lincoln

Remember, nothing that's good works by itself, just to please you.
You've got to *make* the damn thing work.
                    —Thomas A. Edison

Use it or lose it.

                    —American saying popularized by
                    George P. Shultz

Don't put things off—put them over.
                    —Evan Esar

(*See* Action, Get Up and Go.)

Incentive

Strike a dog with a bone and he won't growl.
                    —Irish proverb

Make your top managers rich and they will make you rich.
                    —Robert H. Johnson

Withhold not good from them to whom it is due, when it is in the
power of thine hand to do it.
                    —Proverbs 3:27

If you pay in peanuts, expect to get monkeys.
                    —Anon.

Catch someone doing something right.
                    —Kenneth Blanchard and Spencer
                    Johnson

(*See* Encouragement, Motivation, Praise.)

Industrial Espionage

If the validity of your action depends on its secrecy, better decide
to do something else.
—Harlan Cleveland

Do not let the Evil One persuade you that you can have any secrets
from him.
—Franz Kafka

Let all men know thee, but no man know thee thoroughly: Men
freely ford that see the shallows.
—Benjamin Franklin

Information Age Commitment

The chief executive officer . . . must lead in changing management
philosophy and adapting the style best suited to the age of information. . . . Get started on overcoming computer illiteracy by
learning to operate terminals and access databases. Use a small
computer yourself, daily. Start networking within your organization
by linking various departments and operations to common or shared
databases. Develop a plan for expanding the electronic links to
your field operations, key customers, and key suppliers. . . .
Evaluate the ability and willingness of your managers to make faster
decisions.
—Michael J. Kami

(*See* Computer Etiquette.)

Innovation

The most important matter is to seize a trend, and when we come in with our might it won't matter that we weren't the first. Everyone will think we were.
—Michael C. Bergerac

Concerning any new thing, never consult the man whose life it is about to change.

Never leave well enough alone.*
—Raymond Loewy

*A Loewy dictum: "You take two products with the same function, the same quality, and the same price: the better-looking one will outsell the other."

Don't try to innovate for the future. Innovate for the present!
— Peter F. Drucker

Make sure you generate a reasonable number of mistakes.
—Fletcher Byrom

We ought not to be over-anxious to encourage innovation. In cases of doubtful improvement, an old system must ever have two advantages over a new one: it is established and it is understood.
—Charles Caleb Colton

(See New Ideas.)

Insider Trading

No man should so act as to make a gain out of the ignorance of another.
—Cicero

Prefer a loss to a dishonest gain: the one brings pain at the moment, the other for all time.
—Chilon, 560 B.C.

(*See* Greed.)

Inspiration

Whatever the source of the leader's ideas, he cannot inspire his people unless he expresses vivid goals which in some sense they want. Of course, the more closely he meets their needs, the less "persuasive" he has to be, but in no case does it make sense to speak as if his role is to force submission. Rather it is to strengthen and uplift, to make people feel that they are the origins, not the pawns, of the socio-political system.
—David McClelland

A platoon leader doesn't get his platoon to go by getting up and shouting and saying "I am smarter. I am bigger. I am stronger. I am the leader." He gets men to go along with him because they want to do it for him and they believe in him.
—Dwight D. Eisenhower

(*See* Bosses, Goals, Leadership [Personal].)

Intelligence

The first method for estimating the intelligence of a ruler is to look at the men he has around him.
—Niccolò Machiavelli

Do not assume that the other fellow has intelligence to match yours. He may have more.
                    —Terry-Thomas

Let no day, if possible, pass away without some intellectual gain. . . . It is a wise proverb among the learned, borrowed from the lips and practice of a celebrated painter, *nulla dies sine linea;* let no day pass without one line at least.

   Let the hope of new discoveries, as well as the satisfaction and pleasure of known truths, animate your daily industry.
                    —Isaac Watts

Intelligence (Industrial, Military)

See the land, what it is; and the people that dwelleth therein, whether they be strong or weak, few or many.
                    —Numbers 13:18

Know the character of the enemy and of their principal officers— whether they be rash or cautious, enterprising or timid, whether they fight on principle or from chance.
                    —Vegetius (4th cent.)

(*See* Market Research, Offensive Strategy, Preparation, Surprises.)

Interdependence

It is probably not love that makes the world go around, but rather those mutually supportive alliances through which partners rec-

ognize their dependence on each other for the achievement of shared and private goals. . . . Treat employees like partners and they act like partners.
—Fred T. Allen

Start by teaching the fundamentals. A player's got to know the basics of the game and how to play his position. Next, keep him in line. That's discipline. The men have to play as a team, not a bunch of individuals. . . . Then you've got to care for one another. You've got to *love* each other. . . . Most people call it team spirit.
—Vince Lombardi

(*See* Empowerment, People-Centering, Teamwork.)

Investing

Push yourself hard to ask questions—of yourself, your advisers and anybody trying to sell you an investment. Remember: Nobody is infallible, and there are no dumb questions—only dumb answers.
—Marshall Loeb

Baruch's rules for investing:
Don't buy too many different securities. Better have only a few investments which can be watched.
Always keep a good part of your capital in a cash reserve. Never invest all your funds.
Don't try to be a jack of all investments. Stick to the field you know best.
—Bernard M. Baruch

It is unrealistic to expect to have "up" years consistently. The trick is to nail down substantial profits in good years and preserve capital in bad ones. . . . Condition your emotions to take losses. Taking losses is not a probability, it is a certainty. . . . Some investors are simply born losers. If you know any, invest opposite them.
—Dick Davis

"Keep your accounts on your thumbnail." . . . Your financial life should complement the rest of your life, not dominate it. Invest time up front to make initial financial decisions. But after that, matters should take care of themselves with just a little monitoring from you. Time, Thoreau reminds us, is but the stream we go fishing in. By casting our lines more carefully, we can spend our lives on a higher level, pursuing those things that give us the most genuine reward.
—Candace E. Trunzo

The next time you prepare to buy a stock, it's worth asking yourself why the sellers don't perceive the same value that you do. The answers may not change your mind about buying, but they may make you wait for a better price.
—John J. Curran

The typical question people ask is: "Is this a good investment?" It is better to ask: "Is this a good investment *for me?*"
—Justin Heatter

(*See* Speculation.)

Investment Advisers

Hazard not your wealth on a poor man's advice.
—Anon.

Look for an adviser with a steady, long-term track record . . . who not only has given good advice most of the time, but also has avoided disasters.

Be wary of technicians. The best recognize they are dealing only with probabilities that the market will hew to previous patterns. No one can know what the market will do, because the future depends on how decisions by millions of investors will come together.

Do not put too much trust in anyone. The adviser with the best track record is, in a sense, the most dangerous. His readers may become believers who keep the faith long after the market proves him wrong.
—John C. Boland

Old men are always advising young men to save money. That is bad advice. Don't save every nickel. Invest in yourself. I never saved a dollar until I was 40 years old.
—Henry Ford

(*See* Speculation.)

Involvement

Don't open up a can of worms without knowing how to get the worms back inside.
—Mortimer B. Zuckerman

Have a personal picture of the front and a clear idea of the problems subordinates are having to face. It is the only way in which the commander can keep his ideas permanently up to date and adapted to changing conditions. If he fights his battles as a game of chess, he will become rigidly fixed in academic theory and admiration of his own ideas. Success comes most readily to the commander whose ideas have not been canalized into any one fixed channel, but can develop freely from the conditions around him.
—Field Marshal Erwin Rommel

Tell me and I'll forget; show me and I may remember; involve me and I'll understand.
—Chinese proverb

I try to keep in touch with the details—you can't keep in touch with them all, but you've got to have a feel for what's going on. I also look at the product daily. That doesn't mean you interfere, but it's important occasionally to show the ability to be involved. It shows you understand what's happening.
                                                —Rupert Murdoch

J

Judgment

One cool judgment is worth a thousand hasty councils. The thing to do is to supply light and not heat. At any rate, if it is heat it ought to be white heat and not sputter, because sputtering is apt to spread the fire. There ought, if there is any heat at all, to be that warmth of the heart which makes every man thrust aside his own personal feeling, his own personal interest, and take thought of the welfare and benefit of others.
—Woodrow Wilson

The Commander of an Army neither requires to be a learned explorer of history nor a publicist, but he must be well versed in the higher affairs of state; he must know and be able to judge correctly of traditional tendencies, interests at stake, the immediate questions at issue, and the characters of leading persons; he need not be a close observer of men, a sharp dissecter of human character, but he must know the character, the feelings, the habits, the peculiar faults and inclinations, of those whom he is to command.
—Karl von Clausewitz

K

Kindliness

Three-fourths of the people you will ever meet are hungering and thirsting for sympathy. Give it to them, and they will love you.
— Dale Carnegie

You could have an employee, a customer, or an associate who is seriously ill or who has suffered the loss of a spouse this past year. If there are children involved, remember that they suffer particularly during the holidays. They would really appreciate a gift of an evening or a Saturday afternoon of your time. . . . This is the kind of Christmas present that is really meaningful to your colleagues.
— Letitia Baldrige

Modern corporations should be communities, not battlefields. At their heart lie covenants between executives and employees that rest on shared commitment to ideas, to issues, to values, to goals, and to management processes. Words such as love, warmth, personal chemistry are certainly pertinent.
— Max De Pree

(*See* Gifts [Corporate], Discipline, Tough-Mindedness.)

L

Labor Relations

Treat a thousand dispositions in a thousand ways.
　　　　　—Ovid

[Regarding an organized opposition on his team:] I never let the
four guys who hate me get together with the five who are unde-
cided.
　　　　　—Leo Durocher

　　　If you ride a horse, sit close and tight;
　　　If you ride a man, sit easy and light.
　　　　　—Benjamin Franklin

[On shaking hands:] Put your hand out. See. You've got to hit in
close, deep, where they can feel it. Connect first before they do.
That's the way to make them feel the power.
　　　　　—Nelson A. Rockefeller

Lawyering

If you cannot avoid a quarrel with a blackguard, let your lawyer manage it rather than yourself. No man sweeps his own chimney, but employs a chimney-sweeper who has no objection to dirty work because it is his trade.
　　　　　　　　—Charles Caleb Colton

Don't try to instruct your lawyer. If you do, you've got the wrong lawyer.
　　　　　　　　—John T. Nolan

A lean compromise is better than a fat lawsuit.
　　　　　　　　—English proverb

Never refer to your opponent's "arguments"; he only makes "assertions," and his assertions are always "bald."
　　　　　　　　—Dr. Robert White

Never, never, never on cross examination ask a witness a question you don't know the answer to. . . . Do it, and you'll often get an answer that might wreck your case.
　　　　　　　　—Harper Lee

Be concise for clients. Less is more. Bravura displays only serve to irritate; brevity is what pays the rent.
　　　　　　　　—James C. Freund

If you're weak on the facts pound the law; if you're weak on the law pound the facts; if you're weak on both, pound the table.
　　　　　　　　—Anon.

When you have no basis for an argument, abuse the plaintiff.
　　　　　　　　—Cicero

Leadership (Personal)

The leader must know, must know that he knows, and must be able to make it abundantly clear to those around him that he knows.
—Clarence Randall

You don't lead by pointing and telling people some place to go. You lead by going to that place and making a case.
—Ken Kesey

I tend to use role power—that is, position power—less than many men around me, but have no reluctance to use it. If you really want people to respond to your leadership, you have to have a personal relationship with them. They need to know you're dependable and that you'll be there if they have a problem. That's personal power to me.
—Noreen Haffner

Look over your shoulder now and then to be sure someone's following you.
—Henry Gilmer

(*See* Authority, Bosses, Example, Inspiration, Style.)

Leverage

Don't fight forces. Use them.
—R. Buckminster Fuller

Consider the two levers for moving men—interest and fear.
—Napoleon I

Use your leverage. The worst thing you can possibly do in a deal is seem desperate to make it. That makes the other guy smell blood, and then you're dead. . . . Leverage is having something the other guy wants. Or better yet, needs. Or best of all, simply can't do without.

—Donald J. Trump

(*See* Negotiating.)

Leveraged Buyouts

Get the debt down as fast as possible; sell off anything that it makes economic sense to unload; apply a gimlet eye to capital expenditures and other costs; attack bureaucracy.

—*Fortune* magazine

(*See* Restructuring, Takeovers.)

Listening

Ask employees what's wrong, not what's right.

—An Wang

You have to be willing sometimes to listen to some remarkably bad opinions. Because if you say to someone, "That's the silliest thing I ever heard; get on out of here!"—then you'll never get anything out of that person again, and you might as well have a puppet on a string or a robot.

—John Bryan

We should never pretend to know what we don't know, we should not feel ashamed to ask and learn from people below, and we should listen carefully to the views of the cadres at the lowest levels. Be

a pupil before you become a teacher; learn from the cadres at the lower levels before you issue orders.
                    —Mao Tse-tung

Rather weigh the will of the speaker, than the worth of the words.
                    —English proverb

The impatience we show by making snap decisions or by "shooting from the hip" is unnecessary—and unwise. So is the impatience we show through sarcasm and anger. A former boss of mine constantly admonished, "Slow down. Slow down. Take time to listen." Have patience. Worthwhile work takes time.
                    —James L. Hayes

In some South Pacific cultures, a speaker holds a conch shell as a symbol of a temporary position of authority. Leaders must understand who holds the conch—that is, who should be listened to and when.
                    —Max De Pree

Long View

Wisdom requires the long view. . . . I am reminded of the story of the great French Marshal Lyautey, who once asked his gardener to plant a tree. The gardener objected that the tree was slow-growing and would not reach maturity for a hundred years. The Marshal replied, "In that case, there is no time to lose, plant it this afternoon." Today a world of knowledge—a world of cooperation—a just and lasting peace—may be years away. But we have no time to lose. Let us plant our trees this afternoon.
                    —John F. Kennedy

To elevate the goals of humankind, to achieve high moral purpose, to realize major intended change, leaders must thrust themselves into the most intractable processes and structures of history and ultimately master them.
                    —James MacGregor Burns

It's been said that the foolish man seeks happiness in the distance; the wise man grows it under his feet. Maybe so. But I think you've got to fix the idea of your fulfilled life in your mind. Heaven is for those who plan and act on it.
—Edward Bleier

Know that happiness is a way of travel—not a destination.
—Roy M. Goodman

(*See* Higher Purpose, Vision.)

Loyalty

Stick to a friend a little in the wrong.
—John Randolph

The first thing a young officer must do when he joins the Army is to fight a battle, and that battle is for the hearts of his men. If he wins that battle and subsequent similar ones, his men will follow him anywhere; if he loses it, he will never do any real good.
—Viscount Montgomery of Alamein

O wise man, wash your hands of that friend who associates with your enemies.
—Saadi

Stand with anybody that stands right, stand with him while he is right and part with him when he goes wrong.
—Abraham Lincoln

You must capture and keep the heart of the original and supremely able man before his brain can do its best.
—Andrew Carnegie

Be a friend when people most need one. As movie mogul Lew Wasserman used to advise talent agents: "If an actor is working,

make sure you talk to him at least twice a week. If he is not working, talk to him every day." Helping people will not guarantee that they respond in kind. My experience is that you can count on about one in ten, but this one makes up for the others.
—David Mahoney

The loyalties which center upon number one are enormous. If he trips, he must be sustained. If he makes mistakes, they must be covered. If he sleeps, he must not be wantonly disturbed. If he is no good, he must be pole-axed.
—Winston Churchill

Loyalty (Institutional)

You've got to give loyalty down, if you want loyalty up.
—Donald T. Regan

Talk to people in their own language. If you do it well, they'll say, "God, he said exactly what I was thinking." And when they begin to respect you, they'll follow you to the death.
—Lee J. Iacocca

Put on the "company hat." (Be willing to accept actions that may have a negative impact upon a particular component but are in the best interests of the company as a whole.)
—Reginald H. Jones, quoted by Harry
Levinson and Stuart Rosenthal

Luck

Never underestimate luck.
—An Wang

The uses of pessimism among the lucky can be articulated in terms of Murphy's Law: "If something can go wrong, it will." Never, never assume that you are fortune's darling. Never drop your guard.

—Max Gunther

When fortune calls, quick!—offer her a chair.

—Jewish saying

If heaven drops a date, open your mouth.

—Chinese proverb

Lunchmanship

Never meet anybody after two for lunch. Meet in the morning because you're sharper. Never have long lunches. They're not only boring, but dangerous because of the martinis.

—Joseph P. Kennedy

Unless their biz is show biz, people who must get phone calls at their restaurant tables shouldn't be dining publicly.

—Malcolm Forbes

(*See* Power Lunch.)

M

Mafia Connections

Easy is the way down to the Underworld
by night and by day dark Dis's door
stands open: but to withdraw one's
steps and to make a way out to the
upper air, that's the task, that is
the labour.
—Virgil

Let guilty men remember, their black deeds
Do lean on crutches made of slender reeds.
—John Webster

Don't roll in the mire to please the pigs. Do nothing wrong to
please those who take delight in evil.
—C. H. Spurgeon

(*See* Corruption.)

Magnanimity

Let him show mastery over a fighting foe
And clemency when he has brought him low.
—Horace

Don't do for others what you wouldn't think of asking them to do
for you.
—Josh Billings

(*See* Victory.)

Making Money

The art of getting rich consists not in industry, much less in saving,
but in a better order, in timeliness, in being at the right spot.
—Ralph Waldo Emerson

The shortest and best way to make your fortune is to let people
see clearly that it is in their interests to promote yours.
—Jean de La Bruyère

Let a man start out in life to build something better and sell it
cheaper than it has been built or sold before, let him have the
determination and the money will roll in.
—Henry Ford

He is not fit for riches who is afraid to use them.
—Thomas Fuller

Seek not proud riches, but rather such as thou mayest get justly,
use soberly, distribute cheerfully, and leave contentedly.
—Sir Francis Bacon

Command your wealth, else it will command you.
                          —English proverb

                        (*See* Prosperity.)

Managing

Never try to teach a pig to sing; it wastes your time and it annoys
the pig.
                          —Paul Dickson

        It is not enough to have great qualities;
        We should also have the management of them.
                          —La Rochefoucauld

"The Sy Syms Theory of Management": If a subordinate disappoints
you once, you discount his credibility by 10%; if he disappoints
you twice, it goes down by 30%. The third time you sell out at any
price.
                          —Mortimer R. Feinberg and Aaron
                          Levenstein

Consensus management:
Consensus is what Japan is famous for. . . . In my dealings with
them, they talk a lot about consensus, but there's always one guy
behind the scenes who ends up making the tough decisions. . . .
What's to admire about consensus management anyhow? By its
very nature, it's slow. It can never be daring. There can never be
real accountability—or flexibility. . . . The fun of business for entrepreneurs, big or small, lies in our free enterprise system, not
in the greatest agreement by the greatest number.
                          —Lee J. Iacocca

Crisis management:
You have to take a position, whether you like it or not. The natural inclination is to hide in a hole for a while. But if you don't talk about some of the problems, you create a credibility gap.
—John J. Phelan

Decentralized management:
We spend time with our managers, but we tell them it is their responsibility to run their company. Leaders are developed by challenges.
—James E. Burke

Participative management:
Employee involvement requires participative management. Anyone who has a legitimate reason, who will be affected by a decision, ought to have the feeling that people want to know how he or she feels.
—Donald E. Petersen

(*See* People-Centering.)

Mandates

Great innovations should not be forced on slender majorities.
—Thomas Jefferson

Market Research

Before you build a better mousetrap, it helps to know if there are any mice out there.
—Mortimer B. Zuckerman

Do your homework. Know the product inside and out. Study the product and what has been successful for it in the past. On the other hand, don't use research as a crutch. Remember that the drunkard uses the lamppost for support, not illumination.
                    —David Ogilvy

Agitate the enemy and ascertain the pattern of his movement. Determine his dispositions and so ascertain the field of battle. Probe him and learn where his strength is abundant and where deficient.
                    —Sun Tzu

If you want to hit a moving target, aim where it's going to be, not at where it is.
                    —René Bartos

Don't climb a tree to look for fish.
                    —Chinese proverb

First see the hare . . . then loose the falcon.
                    —Chinese proverb

Though thine enemy seems like a mouse, watch him like a lion.
                    —Italian proverb

All the business of war, and indeed all the business of life, is to endeavor to find out what you don't know by what you do; that's what I called "guessing what was on the other side of the hill."
                    —Arthur Wellesley, Duke of Wellington

Listen to the river and you'll catch a trout.
                    —Irish proverb

(*See* Intelligence [Industrial, Military], Preparation, Testing.)

Mean-Spirited Advice

If you need a friend in Washington, get a dog.
>—Attributed to Harry S. Truman

Media

If you want to be a leader of the people, you must learn to watch events.
>—Benjamin Disraeli

If you don't want to see it in print, or hear it on the radio or television, *do not say it*. Speaking "off the record" will not insure that the statement will not be used. If the reporter goes to the trouble of getting the same information from another source, after you have provided the lead "off the record," he will be ethically able to use it.
>—Art Stevens

Whenever you deal with a reporter make sure that he has an updated fact sheet. You'd be surprised at how many errors are repeated year after year because the reporter's files are out of date. . . . Give him copies of news stories about you that are accurate—this is particularly important when you are involved in a controversy or a breaking news story.
>—Frederick D. Buchstein

Trust no one! Journalists are not your friends. It's not that reporters aren't decent people—they are. They are not interviewing you to meet a new friend, but to get a story. Their job always comes first and don't forget it.
>—Robert L. Woodrum

Don't try to make friends with reporters, but do try to establish a real relationship. If a reporter gets to know you, he can respond to you as an individual instead of as the representative of an institution.
—Herb Schmertz

I'm convinced that if you level with the press, your coverage will be fair and balanced. There's plenty of good and bad in every company. So just share the whole mishmash with them. Believe me, they'll find out the bad stuff anyway. Why not take them behind the scenes and save everyone's time? It's suicidal to hold your cards close to your vest.
—Lee J. Iacocca

Always point your finger at the chest of the person with whom you are being photographed. You will appear dynamic. And no photo editor can crop you from the picture.
—Ken Auletta

[A] rule that I want followed for all of my family, including Pat, Tricia, Julie and David and myself, and that I would advise for everybody else, is *never tape more than the interviewer is going to use.*
—Memo from Richard Nixon to Bob Haldeman

Re: Leaks. Note to White House newcomers to heed John F. Kennedy's rule: "If there is more than one person (yourself) in a room, consider anything said to be on the record and a probable headline in the morning paper."
—Hugh Sidey

Ethics for newspersons:
There are two commandments: do not betray a confidence, and do not knife a comrade. And these two have their practical reason for being. The man who violates a confidence will lose his sources of

news; the man who double-crosses a colleague will, on some bloody tomorrow, find himself naked and helpless.
—Stanley Walker

(*See* Press Conferences, Public Relations, Television Appearances.)

Meetings

Ask yourself the question that will occur to everyone summoned to attend: Is this gathering really necessary? To decide the answer, you have to be clear about your purpose, for that will determine what kind of meeting, if any, you should have. . . .

When you convene the troops be sure to tell them why you are getting together. Besides knowing what to expect, they will know what to prepare. . . . Draw up an agenda and circulate it well in advance—two days beforehand at a minimum.
—Walter Kiechel III

If we are going to intervene at a meeting, we must do so at the right moment, prepare for what we want to say, speak up at the crucial point when our intervention will be heard and listened to, make sure that attention is paid. Otherwise, it's best to remain silent. It is better to do nothing than do something badly.
—Michael Korda

If you are running a meeting, remember that few people like to be called on "cold" to report on their activities. If you want someone to speak, give him or her a little introduction before passing the ball.

—Roger Varney

Minimize ambiguity. (Change the functions of the vice-chairman and the corporate executive staff, and ensure that people know the purpose of a meeting—decision-making meetings versus review meetings versus communication meetings.)
—Reginald H. Jones

Better debate a question without settling it than settle a question
without debating it.
                              —Joseph Joubert

Memos

                    Damn your writing.
                    Mind your fighting.
                    —Attributed to
                        General Sir Archibald P. Wavell,
                        to "a British general
                        who rose to high command"

Do not engage in any paper wars.
                              —Florence Nightingale

You don't have to have a piece of paper to know where you are
going and to act.
                              —Paul H. Nitze

I am a strong believer in transacting official business by The Written
Word.
                              —Winston Churchill

If you don't know what to do with many of the papers piled on
your desk, stick a dozen colleagues' initials on 'em, and pass them
along. When in doubt, route.
                              —Malcolm Forbes

                    (See Orders.)

Mistakes

You've got to have an atmosphere where people can make mistakes. If we're not making mistakes, we're not going anywhere. The scientific method is designed for mistakes.
—Gordon Forward

It never bothers me for people to make a mistake if they had a reason for what they did. If they can tell me, "I thought this and reasoned so, and came to that decision," if they obviously went through a reasonable thought process to get where they did, even if it didn't turn out right, that's OK. The ones you want to watch out for are those who can't even tell you why they did what they did.
—Frank Gaines

If a manager makes the same mistake three times, fire him.
—An Wang

Morale

In all forms of warfare the loser is beaten in spirit before he is beaten in fact. Never let respect become intimidation.
—David J. Rogers

Remember that morale always filters down from the top. It reflects the attitudes of people at every level—especially the attitudes of supervisors toward their own jobs and toward the people they supervise.
—Louis B. Lundborg

We believe that if you want high efficiency and productivity, a close cordial relationship with your employees which leads to high morale is necessary. Sometimes it is more important to generate

a sense of affinity than anything else and sometimes you must make decisions that are, technically, irrational. You can be totally rational with a machine. But if you work with people, sometimes logic often has to take a backseat to understanding.
—Akio Morita

(*See* People-Centering, Teamwork, Understanding.)

Morality

When we are trying to decide whether a leader is a good leader or a bad one, the question to ask is: "Is he with the Ten Commandments or is he against them?" Then you can determine if the leader is a true messiah or another Stalin.
—Isaac Bashevis Singer

I believe deeply that every occupant of the White House . . . has one profound duty to the nation; to exert moral leadership. The President of the United States should stand, visible and uncompromising, for what is right and decent—in government, in the business community, in the private lives of the citizens. For decency is one of the main pillars of a sound civilization. An immoral nation invites its own ruin.
—Dwight D. Eisenhower

I tell my people, "Don't play games. Don't lie to me. Don't lie for me. Don't do me any favors. Play it straight."
—Robert A. Pritzker

If you happen to be sitting near people whose voices you hear clearly and they are discussing something sensitive to you or your company, stop them—quietly, politely, and quickly. Explain that you are with such-and-such a company and that it would be preferable for them to lower their voices or change the subject. . . . This is a situation in which a sense of morality should prevail.
—Letitia Baldrige

If you want to be St. Francis of Assisi, you should not head a public company.
                              —Jean Riboud

Look with suspicion upon such slogans as "You can't argue with success." You can, and should. There are honorable ways of becoming a success, and ways that are legitimate but not quite honorable. The profit motive must be governed by moral restrictions. "Let the buyer beware" is a poor business philosophy for a social order allegedly based upon man's respect for his fellow man. Let the seller beware, too. A free-enterprise system not founded upon personal morality will ultimately lose its freedom. Apply the time-tested principles of good family living to the family of man.
                              —Sam Levenson

(*See* Ethics in Business, Honesty.)

Motivation

Remember, the best incentive in business is the sound of the boss's footsteps.
                              —Business adage

If you want a man to be for you, never let him feel he is dependent on you. Make him feel you are in some way dependent on him.
                              —General George C. Marshall

When Sam Snead was asked how to putt, he answered: "Putt for a hundred dollars."
                              —Quoted by Bob Schieffer

Don't drive your horse with the whip—use the oat bag.
                              —Russian proverb

Keep in mind that the people working in your company are interested in the same rewards that you are.
                              —Milton Moscowitz

Don't claim credit for any success you may get. People in trouble need credit much more than you do.
                                    —Brian Urquhart

I am your king. You are a Frenchman. There is the enemy. Charge!
                                    —Henry IV, Battle of Ivry, 1590

In motivating people, you've got to engage their minds and their hearts. It is good business to have an employee feel part of the entire effort. . . . I motivate people, I hope, by example—and perhaps by excitement, by having provocative ideas to make others feel involved.
                                    —Rupert Murdoch

When there's a collective fear, one person can bring confidence to the group. If you do things with a question mark, everyone is going to have a question mark. The role of a leader is not to challenge people, but to get them to challenge themselves.
                                    —Michel Roux

There is only one way under high Heaven to get anybody to do anything. Did you ever stop to think of that? Yes, just one way. And that is by making the other person want to do it. Remember, there is no other way.
                                    —Dale Carnegie

(*See* Encouragement, Goading, Inspiration, People-Centering, Praise, Threats.)

Mystery

The leader of men in warfare can show himself to his followers only through a mask, a mask that he must make for himself, but a mask made in such form as will mark him to men of his time and place as the leader they want and need.
                                    —John Keegan

Never reveal all of yourself to other people; hold back something in reserve so that people are never quite sure if they really know you.

—Michael Korda

Mix a little mystery with everything, for mystery arouses veneration.

—Baltasar Gracián

The power to command has never meant the power to remain mysterious.

—Marshal Ferdinand Foch

There can be no power without mystery. There must always be a "something" which others cannot altogether fathom, which puzzles them, stirs them, and rivets their attention. . . . Nothing more enhances authority than silence. It is the crowning virtue of the strong, the refuge of the weak, the modesty of the proud, the pride of the humble, the prudence of the wise, and the sense of fools.

—Charles de Gaulle

Always mystify, mislead and surprise the enemy if possible.

—General Thomas J. "Stonewall" Jackson

(*See* Charisma.)

N

Negotiating

Make your enemy your friend.
> —English proverb

Endeavor to oppose without exasperating; to practice temporary hostility, without producing enemies for life.
> —Samuel Johnson

These four points define a straightforward method of negotiation that can be used under almost any circumstances. Each point deals with a basic element of negotiation, and suggests what you should do about it.

People: Separate the people from the problem.

Interests: Focus on interests, not positions.

Options: Generate a variety of possibilities before deciding what to do.

Criteria: Insist that the result be based on some objective standard.
> —Roger Fisher and William Ury

Whether it's a labor negotiation, an acquisition, or a real-estate deal, don't deceive yourself into believing that just because it's negotiable, it has to be negotiated. . . . Deals seldom get worse

when you walk away from the table. Be prepared to walk away from the table . . . and mean it. You'll be able to go back to the table and get even better terms.
                    —Harvey Mackay

Never forget the power of silence, the massively disconcerting pause that goes on and on and may at last induce an opponent to babble and backtrack nervously.
                    —Lance Morrow

When you want something from a person, think first of what you can give him in return. Let him think that it's he who is coming off best. But all the time make sure it is you in the end.
                    —Sir Robert Oppenheimer

The correct strategy for Americans negotiating with Japanese or other foreign clients is a Japanese strategy: ask questions. When you think you understand, ask more questions. Carefully feel for pressure points. If an impasse is reached, don't pressure. Suggest a recess or another meeting.
                    —John L. Graham and Roy A.
                    Herberger, Jr.

Don't paint people into a corner. This makes them dangerous, paranoid and obstinate.
                    —Brian Urquhart

Never play cat and mouse games if you're a mouse.
                    —Don Addis, quoted by Paul Dickson

Prepare by knowing your walkaway and by building the number of variables you can work with during the negotiation. Everyone agrees about the walkaway. Whether you're negotiating an arms deal with the Russians, a labor agreement with the UAW, or a contract you can't afford to lose, you need to have a walkaway: a combination of price, terms, and deliverables that represents the least you will accept. Without one, you have no negotiating road map.

                    —Thomas C. Keiser

(*See* Contracts, Leverage, Perks, Takeovers.)

Nepotism

Never hire your client's children.
                    —David Ogilvy

> Spurn not the nobly-born
> With love affected,
> Nor treat with virtuous scorn,
> The well-connected.
>   —W. S. Gilbert

What you have inherited from your father, you must earn over
again for yourselves, or it will not be yours.
                    —Goethe

(*See* Favoritism.)

Networking

How to network:
  Meet as many people as you can.
  When you meet someone, tell him what you do. "Networking is
    low-cost advertising."
  Don't do business while networking. Make a date to meet your
    contact for drinks or lunch.
  Give and get. You can't always be a buyer. Do favors. They're
    like a savings account.
  Make friends even when you don't need them.
                    —Steve Fishman

The story is about an old, crusty fisherman who would walk out to
the end of the pier each day with his old rod, rusty reel, bucket
and a stick that was snapped off at the 10 inch mark. Each day he
would cast his line and catch fish. When he measured them against

his stick, he would throw back the ones that were bigger than 10 inches and keep the ones smaller than 10 inches. Since this was the opposite of what most fishermen would do, someone asked him for his reason. This old fisherman stated: " 'Cause my frying pan is only 10 inches."

When it comes to networking, this fisherman is me. That fisherman is you. And we all need to go out and buy a bigger frying pan.

—Peter B. Stark

Always have distinguished friends. Never have fools for friends, they are of no use.

—Benjamin Disraeli

Start a file of your friends and acquaintances, what they're doing, and where they are. Keep it updated. You should be continually asking yourself: Who might like to hear from me, and whom can I help? Serendipity works in your favor, if you keep in touch.

—David Mahoney

(*See* Contacts.)

New Ideas

The best way to have a good idea is to have a lot of ideas.

—Dr. Linus Pauling

You must find the ideas that have some promise in them . . . it isn't enough to just have ideas, they must be finally ideas worth having and fruitful.

—George E. Woodbury

If you can't write your idea on the back of my calling card, you don't have a clear idea.

—David Belasco

Never, never rest contented with any circle of ideas, but always be certain that a wider one is still possible.
—Richard Jefferies

We should always have in our heads one free and open corner, where we can give place, or lodging as they pass, to the ideas of our friends. It really becomes unbearable to converse with men whose brains are divided up into well-filled pigeon-holes, where nothing can enter from outside. Let us have hospitable hearts and minds.
—Joseph Joubert

Acquire a government over your ideas, that they may come down when they are called, and depart when they are bidden.
—Isaac Watts

The best ideas come as jokes. Make your thinking as funny as possible.
—David Ogilvy

When an idea is too weak to stand the test of simple expression, it should be dropped.
—Marquis de Vauvenargues

You can only acquire really useful general ideas by first acquiring particular ideas. . . . You cannot make bricks without straw.
—Arnold Bennett

I have found out one thing and that is, if you have an idea, and it is a good idea, if you only stick to it you will come out all right.
—Cecil Rhodes

Too many companies get stuck with a sexy idea that has no practical application. I get with my people and say to them, "Now let's take this idea and see where we can go with it." Then I start to play it back and forth with them, and before you know it one of them has turned it into an idea with real business potential. Just that fact that you get in and get interested and talk with them about their ideas—that stimulates them and excites them about what they're doing.

—Paul Charlap

(*See* Experimentation.)

Obedience

The leader must himself believe that willing obedience always beats forced obedience, and that he can get this only by really knowing what should be done. Thus he can secure obedience from his men because he can convince them that he knows best, precisely as a good doctor makes his patients obey him.
　　　　—Xenophon

There is no act more moral between men than that of rule and obedience. Woe to him that claims obedience when it is not due; woe to him that refuses it when it is!
　　　　—Thomas Carlyle

If you would secure obedience, show affection. It is a power that succeeds, when others fail.
　　　　—Thomas Fuller

A man must require just and reasonable things if he would see the scales of obedience properly trimmed. From orders which are improper, springs resistance which is not easily overcome.
　　　　—St. Basil

157

Let them obey that know not how to rule.
>   —Duke of York, in Shakespeare's
>   2 *Henry IV*

(*See* Clarity, Discipline, Fear, Orders.)

Objectivity

Whether you are managing an organization or trying to manage your own life, your ability to cope successfully, to succeed—even survive—depends upon *objectivity*. The Japanese word *sunao* translates roughly as "the untrapped mind." It describes the ability to see the world as it is, not as one wishes it to be. Konosuke Matsushita, the pioneering Japanese industrialist, says that the *sunao* spirit is essential for success at managing today. "Without it," he writes, "one can enjoy neither genuine success in management nor genuine happiness in life."
>   —Arnold Brown and Edith Weiner

Offensive Strategy

Probe with bayonets; if you encounter mush, proceed; if you encounter steel, withdraw.
>   —Attributed to V. I. Lenin

A war should only be undertaken with forces proportionate to the obstacles to be overcome.
>   —Napoleon I

Never attempt an offensive unless you're superior to your competitor in some way. "The offensive, always the offensive" is an attitude that nearly got the French defeated in World War I. "The offensive almost always but not if it's absurd" is a better one. Even though you can't win without taking to the offense, if you're up against a competitor who is more powerful than you in your business and your markets, for the time being at least you have no choice but to take a defensive stance.

—David J. Rogers

When an advancing enemy crosses water do not meet him at the water's edge. It is advantageous to allow half his force to cross and then strike.

—Sun Tzu

Keep the enemy in the dark about where and when our forces will attack.

—Mao Tse-tung

(*See* Concentration of Forces, Deception, Surprises.)

Office Etiquette

Men and women executives should not kiss each other in public. Even air-kissing—the grazing of two cheeks in a fake kiss—looks particularly ridiculous in the workplace. And of course groping is strictly verboten.

—Letitia Baldrige

(*See* Courtesy.)

Office Grapevine

The office grapevine is 75% to 95% accurate and provides managers and staff with better information than formal communications, ac-

cording to a recent study. Rather than ignore or try to repress the grapevine, it's crucial for executives to tune into it.
—Carol Hymowitz

Protect Informants: As you demonstrate your commitment by listening and fixing things, you will hear more and more unvarnished truth, often drifting in through side channels. Use it with care, and make sure, by using your own network, that no informant gets burned by an irate supervisor. And if a supervisor ever comes down on someone who was candid with you about a problem, remove him or her from managerial responsibility on the spot.
—Tom Peters

(*See* Communication.)

Office Politics

Consider this kind of "office politicking" a cardinal sin:
If anyone tries to line up other managers to back his pet project in return for a quid pro quo later, or if anyone tries to force a man junior to him to give anything other than his honest opinion, he does so in peril of losing his job.
—Harold Geneen

Office Romance

Don't play Dear Abby and don't be Dr. Ruth. You're not supposed to have the answers to romantic questions. . . . You cannot fire people because they fall in love, but it is incumbent upon you to remind employees that you can fire people who are so preoccupied with their personal lives that they fail to fulfill their job responsi-

bilities. . . . And you do have the right to keep your office from becoming the Dating Game.
—Lois Wyse

Anytime you have more power than the person you're asking out, you're open to charges of sexual harassment. If you have genuine feelings for a woman you work with, make it clear that the offer can be refused without any job ramifications.
—Stephen Andersen

(*See* Sex.)

Opponents

Make the opponent yours. Absorb and incorporate his thinking into your own. Become one with him so you know him perfectly and can be one step ahead of his every movement.
—Ueshiba Sensei

Gain from your opponents without sacrificing your own strength.
—Japanese proverb

Think not to contend with a man mightier than thou.
—Homer

Forget your opponents; always play against par.
—Sam Snead

Divide the fire, and you will the sooner put it out.
—Publilius Syrus

(*See* Competition.)

Optimism

The day may dawn when fair play, love for one's fellow man, respect for justice and freedom, will enable tormented generations to march forth serene and triumphant from the hideous epoch in which we have to dwell. Meanwhile, never flinch, never weary, never despair.
> —Winston Churchill

> Lay aside life-harming heaviness
> And entertain a cheerful disposition.
> > —Bushy, in Shakespeare's
> > *King Richard II*

Orders

Remember, gentlemen, an order that can be misunderstood will be misunderstood.
> —Helmuth von Moltke ("the Elder")

I hope that you will make sure that when you give an order it is obeyed with promptness. . . . There is always a danger that anything contrary to Service prejudices will be obstructed and delayed.
> —Winston Churchill
> Note for Secretary of State for War,
> 1940

A commander must train his subordinate commanders, and his own staff, to work and act on verbal orders. Those who cannot be trusted to act on clear and concise verbal orders, but want everything in writing, are useless.
> —Viscount Montgomery of Alamein

When I give difficult orders, I like to do so in person, so that I can meet my soldiers' eyes.
> —Unidentified Israeli general, quoted by
> John Keegan

Many years ago a VP at one of the networks said, "Women will never be leaders because they can't give orders." . . . Today, giving orders is no longer in style. . . . Women, including myself, have mainly been able to lead by inspiring and encouraging people to work on solutions—not by throwing their weight around. In this sense we're really in step, as a group, with what's being demanded of managers today.
> —Muriel Fox

(*See* Clarity, Memos, Obedience.)

Organization

"Niche or be niched." . . . If you are not configuring your organization to become a fast-changing, high-value-adding creator of niche markets, you are simply out of step.
> —Tom Peters

Both informed observation and research show that in every organization there is a group of members whose views mean most. This group is the executive core. . . . A chief executive must manage the balance of power within this group so that its goals are compatible with the available organizational resources while not excluding key members. Lyndon Johnson provided an especially pithy example of this principle. When asked why he put up with the extraordinary nuisance of an elderly, cantankerous J. Edgar Hoover, he said: "Well, it's probably better to have him inside the tent pissing out than outside pissing in."
> —James L. Bower

Avoid having too rigid an organization. . . . I've often thought that after you get organized, you ought to throw the chart away.
          —David Packard

Nothing is particularly hard if you divide it into small jobs.
          —Henry Ford

One may hit the mark, another blunder; but heed not these distinctions. Only from the alliance of the one, working with and through the other, are great things born.
          —Antoine de Saint-Exupéry

(*See* Hierarchy.)

P

Packaging

Emerson said that if you build a better mousetrap the world will beat a path to your door, and that may have been true then . . . but it's not true now. No one will come. You have to package and promote that mousetrap. Then they will come.
— Charles Gillette

Marshal thy notions into a handsome method. One will carry twice more weight trussed and packed up in bundles where it lies untowardly flapping hanging around his shoulders. Things orderly fardled up under heads are most portable.
— Thomas Fuller

Paternalism

"Mind Your Own Business, Boss!" . . . Don't try to tell your employees that they should stop smoking altogether, even if you are convinced it would be good for them. Of course, do not presume to approve or disapprove of their sexual preferences. By the same token, don't accept that you must protect them from the rudeness of strangers. Keep in mind that every time you speak up outside of the confines of work-related matters, you weaken the power and influence you wield there.

—Andrew S. Grove

[Japanese] workers are . . . sensing that the system of lifetime employment isn't what it used to be and that self-interest may be the best policy. "The relations between companies and individuals are becoming cool," says Haruyuki Kawamoto, who . . . left Toyota Motor Corp. after 16 years and joined BMW's Japanese subsidiary as an assistant senior manager. "If you count on corporate paternalism, you will be a loser."

—*Wall Street Journal*

(*See* People-Centering.)

Patience

Do not be impatient, for, as Emerson says, "No one can cheat you out of ultimate success but yourself."

—Andrew Carnegie

An admirer once remarked to the great pianist Paderewski on how much patient effort he must have invested to perfect his art. Paderewski's casual reply is a classic: "Everyone has patience. I learned to use mine." If they are to perfect their art, managers, too, must have patience. It is frustrating to wait for a plan to come to fruition, a promising subordinate to develop, a team to take shape, a crisis to be resolved. But such matters will yield to patience—and sustained effort.

—James L. Hayes

Sit down and discuss a responsibility or task with a subordinate and have the subordinate tell you what a reasonable goal and time frame are. If you agree, you are going to have to wait it out. If

necessary you are going to have to sit on your hands, but you are going to have to give him a chance to do the job.
—Bill Kaufman

(*See* Frustration.)

Patriotism

We should behave toward our country as women behave toward the men they love. A loving wife will do anything for her husband except stop criticizing and trying to improve him. We should cast the same affectionate but sharp glance at our country.
—J. B. Priestley

Peacekeeping

Who desires peace, let him prepare for war.
—Vegetius (4th cent.)

If you would preserve peace, then prepare for peace.
—Barthélemy Enfantin

People-Centering

My philosophy is that you can't do anything yourself. Your people have to do it.
—Beth Pritchard

Always recognize that human individuals are ends, and do not use
them as means to your end.
                              —Immanuel Kant

When dealing with people, let us remember we are not dealing
with creatures of logic. We are dealing with creatures of emotion,
creatures bustling with prejudices and motivated by pride and
vanity.
                              —Dale Carnegie

Everyone has an invisible sign hanging from his neck saying Make
Me Feel Important! Never forget this message when working with
people.
                              —Mary Kay Ash

(See Control, Empowerment, Encouragement, Morale,
Paternalism, Praise, Productivity, Teamwork, Understanding.)

Performance

Act impeccably! Perform every act as if it were the only thing in
the world that mattered. . . . It's an old Zen principle—you put
your whole soul and being and life into the act you're performing.
In Zen archery your entire being wills the arrow into the bull's-
eye with an invisible force. It's not a question of winning or even
caring, it's making the everyday acts we all perform important to
ourselves. No matter how small the talk, we have to teach ourselves
that it *matters*.
                              —Michael Korda

Put your best foot forward.
                              —William Congreve

Deliver the goods. You can't con people, at least not for long. You
can create excitement, you can do wonderful promotion and get

all kinds of press, and you can throw in a little hyperbole. But if you don't deliver the goods, people will eventually catch on.
—Donald J. Trump

(*See* Action, Capability, Credibility, Productivity, Proficiency.)

Perks

Remember that everything is negotiable. If you don't ask, you won't get. And if you're rebuffed, you're no worse off than you were before. Experienced executives, however, do not let greed overwhelm their common sense.
—James R. Baehler

(*See* Negotiating.)

Perseverance

Keep busy; idleness is the strength of bad habits. Do not give up the struggle when you have broken your resolution once, twice, ten times, a thousand times. That only shows how much need there is for you to strive . . . one can but try. "Genius is divine *perseverance.*" Genius I cannot claim nor even extra brightness but perseverance *all* can have.
—Woodrow Wilson

Persevere and preserve yourselves for better circumstances.
—Virgil

Never *play* with an uprising, but once it has begun, be firm in the knowledge that you have to *carry it through to the end*. . . . Once the uprising has begun, one must act with the utmost *decisiveness*

and go over *to the offensive*. . . . One must strive daily for small victories . . . in order to maintain at all costs *moral superiority*.
                                        —V. I. Lenin

(*See* Determination.)

Perspective

Do not worry about holding high position; worry rather about playing your proper role.
                                        —Confucius

Never make troubles of trifles.
                                        —English proverb

All good leaders must have the ability to keep their perspective. I always tell my clients how the Roman emperors dealt with this problem when they ruled the world. When a general returned to Rome from a great victory on the battlefield, he was honored with a tumultuous parade. In the procession the conqueror was preceded by trumpeters, his soldiers, the treasure and captives from the conquered lands, and received the cheers of the citizens. The conqueror rode in a golden chariot with a slave, who whispered in his ear: "Remember, you are a mortal man, all glory is fleeting."
                                        —Robert L. Woodrum

(*See* Humility.)

Persuasion

Remember the prophet Isaiah. Come let us reason together. Telling a man to go to hell and making him go there are two different things.
—Lyndon B. Johnson

Would you persuade, speak of interest, not of reason.
—Benjamin Franklin

He who rules must humor full as much as he commands.
—George Eliot

Action springs out of what we fundamentally desire . . . and the best piece of advice which can be given to would-be persuaders, whether in business, in the home, in the school, in politics, is: first, arouse in the other person an eager want.
—Harry A. Overstreet

(*See* Argument.)

Pessimism

You are sad in the midst of every blessing. Take care that Fortune does not observe—or she will call you ungrateful.
—Martial

One must have the courage of one's pessimism.
—Ian McEwan

(*See* Attitude, Optimism.)

Philanthropy

The only noble use of surplus wealth is this: That it be regarded as a sacred trust, to be administered by its possessor, into whose hands it flows, for the highest good of the people.
                    —Andrew Carnegie

A . . . key axiom in giving is a simple one—namely, "you can't take it with you." Hence, you had better use it intelligently while you are on this earth. . . . One associate recently phrased it somewhat differently, saying, "you'll never see a hearse with a luggage rack."
                    —David Rockefeller

(*See* Corporate Giving.)

Planning

Saddle your dreams before you ride 'em.
                    —Mary Webb

Premeditate your speeches; words once flown
Are in the hearer's power, not your own.
                    —Anon.

Plan backwards (set objectives and trace back to see how to achieve them, even though you may discover there is no way to get there and you will have to adjust the objectives). Plan forward (to see where your steps will take you. It is seldom clear and is certainly not always intuitive).
                    —Donald H. Rumsfeld

If you are planning for one year, grow rice. If you are planning for
20 years, grow trees. If you are planning for centuries, grow men.
                    —Chinese proverb

(*See* Preparation, Strategic Planning.)

Playing to Win

Never play not to lose; always play to win.
                    —David Mahoney

[A general] must have "character," which simply means that he
knows what he wants and has the courage and determination to
get it. He must have a genuine interest in, and a real knowledge
of humanity, the raw materials of his trade, and, most vital of all,
he must have what we call the fighting spirit, the will to win.
                    —General Sir Archibald P. Wavell

To be a winner, a man must play to win. This does not mean that
he must be ruthless, cruel, harsh or treacherous. On the contrary,
the better his reputation for integrity, honesty, and decency, the
better his chances of victory will be in the long run. But from time
to time every businessman, like every poker player, is offered a
choice between certain loss or bluffing within the legal rules of the
game. If he is not resigned to losing, if he wants to rise in his
company and industry, then in such a crisis he will bluff—and bluff
hard.
                    —Albert Carr

(*See* Character, Determination.)

Policy-Making

Policy-making is not as easy as slurping down cabbage soup. Caution should be combined with decisiveness. As the saying goes, before going into the room, make sure you can get out again.
                    —Yegor Ligachev

[The American President] need not make a fetish of consistency but he must avoid confusion or the appearance of deception. He will in most cases, therefore, adopt his own policies as precedents and consider his own statements as binding, whether they were contained in an informal answer to a press conference question or in a formal document of state.
                    —Theodore Sorensen

(*See* Credibility, Prudence.)

Politics

Kamin's Sixth Law: When attempting to predict legislative moves by a politician, never be misled by what is said; instead, watch what is done.
                    —Arthur Bloch

Get a good issue and stick with it, hammer away on it, and never let the opposition cause you to lose your temper. Stay on the offensive.
                    —John Tower

People expect Byzantine, Machiavellian logic from politicians. But the truth is simple. Trial lawyers learn a good rule: "Don't decide what you don't have to decide." That's not evasion, it's wisdom.
                    —Mario Cuomo

The art of politics is not to believe what your friends tell you, but to understand what they cannot tell you.
—Jonas Savimbi

[On businessmen who enter politics:] You're criticized daily in print and in speeches. You have to have a thick skin. That's hard for CEO's who have been in a cocoon, flattered by senior managers, protected by lawyers and a PR department. There's no flattery in Washington. Many subordinates have their own agendas, different from the boss's. . . . We all gripe about government. If business people want it to get better, they have to get into it.
—Donald T. Regan

(*See* Power Curve.)

Power

Use power to help people. For we are given power not to advance our own purposes nor to make a great show in the world, nor a name. There is but one just use of power and it is to serve people.
—From a prayer cited by George Bush
in his Inaugural Address, 1989

Power is the ability to prevail—and if you have it, you must, at the same time, assiduously avoid taking the privilege seriously. Best not even to acknowledge it.
—Barry Diller

If a man can accept a situation in a place of power with the thought that it's only temporary, he comes out all right. But when he thinks that he is the cause of the power, that can be his ruination.
—Harry S. Truman

. . . the ability to problem-solve is power. The ability to interact— to effect conciliation, compromise, team spirit . . . that is power. . . . You don't have to conform to some stereotype of a tough-minded

executive in order to have and use power. In the final analysis you have to be yourself.
> —Colombe Nicholas

Always remember to keep your swash buckled.
> —Gerald Lee Steese, quoted by Paul Dickson

Any time you think you have influence, try ordering around someone else's dog.
> —The Cockle Bar

(*See* Action, Decision-Making, Ego Trips, Hubris.)

Power Curve

As a general marches at the head of his troops, so ought wise politicians . . . to march at the head of affairs. . . . They ought not to wait the event, to know what measures to take; but the measures which they have taken ought to produce the event.
> —Demosthenes

Being a President is like riding a tiger . . . keep on riding or be swallowed. A President is either constantly on top of events or . . . events will soon be on top of him.
> —Harry S. Truman

(*See* Action, Politics.)

Power Lunch

Don't be afraid to call: No one was ever offended by an invitation. But do be certain to make the call yourself.

No first invitation should ever be extended secretary to secretary.

Never ask (or have your secretary ask) a guest where he or she wants to eat. The burden of choice is not the guest's.

Never, never, never invite someone to a club that permits discrimination, sexual, religious, or racial.

Don't hurry a waiter in order to show your power.

—Lois Wyse

(*See* Lunchmanship.)

Pragmatism

In seeking to upset the enemy's balance, a commander must not lose his own balance. He needs to have the quality which Voltaire described as the keystone of Marlborough's success—"that calm courage in the midst of tumult, that serenity of soul in danger, which the English call a cool head." But to it he must add the quality for which the French have found the most aptly descriptive phrase—"le sens du praticable." The sense of what is possible, and what is not possible—tactically and administratively. The combination of both these two "guarding" qualities might be epitomised as the power of cool calculation. The sands of history are littered with the wrecks of finely conceived plans that expired for want of this ballast.

—B. H. Liddell Hart

The most successful businessman is the man who holds onto the old just as long as it is good, and grabs the new just as soon as it is better.

—Robert P. Vanderpoel

(*See* Coolness Under Fire.)

Praise

If you want to give a man credit, put it in writing. If you want to give him hell, do it on the phone.
  —Charles Beacham

Hereafter, if you should observe an occasion to give your officers and friends a little more praise than is their due, and confess more fault than you can justly be charged with, you will only become the sooner for it, a great captain. Criticizing and censuring almost everyone you have to do with, will diminish friends, increase enemies, and thereby hurt your affairs.
  —Benjamin Franklin
  Letter to John Paul Jones

  When someone praises you, be judge
    alone:
  Trust not men's judgment of you, but
    your own.
      —Dionysius Cato

A basic rule for managers is "Pass the pride down." People like to create when they can earn recognition for their ideas. When a good idea surfaces, the creator's immediate superiors should show prompt appreciation.
  —James L. Hayes

One of my favorite sayings is that in this company we stack every bit of criticism between two layers of praise. I think this is a more diplomatic, concerned approach.
  —Mary Kay Ash

  (See Criticism, Encouragement, Motivation.)

Preparation

Let your loins be girded about, and your lights burning.
—Luke 12:35

The commander must decide how he will fight the battle *before it begins*. He must then decide how he will use the military effort at his disposal to force the battle to swing the way he wishes it to go; he must make the enemy dance to his tune from the beginning and not vice versa.
—Viscount Montgomery of Alamein

We should make war without leaving anything to chance, and in this especially consists the talent of a general.
—Maurice de Saxe

Something must be left to chance; nothing is sure in a Sea Fight beyond all others.
—Admiral Horatio Nelson
Plan of attack before Trafalgar, 1805

(*See* Intelligence [Industrial, Military], Market Research, Planning, Reserve.)

Press Conferences

Prepare/Rehearse. You set the agenda. Before meeting with the press determine your objectives. Write down the two or three main points you want to make and stick to them during the interview. Anticipate the tough questions and practice your answers with your staff.

When asked a question by a reporter remember: *Answer the question you wish you had been asked*. Make the points you want to make and stick to your agenda. Never say "No comment," which implies you have something to hide. If you can't answer the question, say so.

Always assume every remark you make is "on the record."

Think in print. Casual off the cuff remarks and jokes have no place in an interview. The joke you heard at lunch today about the Mayor may look very embarrassing in print.
                    —Robert L. Woodrum

Don't let a reporter put words into your mouth unless you agree with the question. Do not repeat the reporter's terminology, because what you are doing is making his quote your quote.
                    —Art Stevens

(See Media, Public Relations.)

Principles

It's important that people know what you stand for. It's equally important that they know what you won't stand for.
                    —Mary Waldrop

Act wisely, upon solid principles, and from true motives, but keep them to yourself, and never talk sententiously.
                    —Lord Chesterfield

If we don't stand for something, we will fall for anything.
                    —Irene Dunne

(See Expediency.)

Priorities

The older I get, the more wisdom I find in the ancient rule of taking first things first—a process which often reduces the most complex human problems to manageable proportions.
—Dwight D. Eisenhower

We know that we are not omnipotent and that we must set priorities. We cannot "pay any price" or "bear any burden." We must discriminate; we must be prudent and careful; we must respond in ways appropriate to the challenge and engage our power only when very important strategic stakes are involved.
—George P. Shultz

You have to be able to set priorities. I always remember my father said, "Chuck, your health comes first; without that you have nothing. The family comes second. Your business comes third. You better recognize and organize those first two, so that you can take care of the third."
—Charles Knight

Control your own time. Don't let it be done for you. If you are working off the in-box that is fed to you, you are probably working on the priority of others.
—Donald H. Rumsfeld

Problem-Solving

Be a part of the solution to avoid being a part of the problem. Assistants and workers who love to deposit "insoluble" problems at the feet of their employers like dead kittens will always remain in assistant positions.
—Liz Smith

Never underestimate a problem or your ability to cope with it. Realize that the problem you are facing has been faced by millions of human beings. You have untapped potential for dealing with a problem if you will take the problem and your own undeveloped, unchanneled powers seriously. Your reaction to the problem, as much as the problem itself, will determine the outcome. I have seen people face the most catastrophic problems with a positive mental attitude, turning their problems into creative experience. They turned their scars into stars.
                    —Robert H. Schuller

Know whether a problem is worth solving. There will always be dark days, but if your conviction of the value of the problem is such that you go right ahead in spite of the difficulties, the chances are that you will achieve success in the end.

Problems are the price of progress. Don't bring me anything but trouble. Good news weakens me.
                    —Charles F. Kettering

Approach each new problem not with a view of finding what you hope will be there, but to get the truth, the realities that must be grappled with. You may not like what you find. In that case you are entitled to try to change it. But do not deceive yourself as to what you do find to be the facts of the situation.
                    —Bernard M. Baruch

[How to think about a problem:] The first step is to make the problem specific. . . . The second step is to form theories freely of how to rid yourself of that burden. . . . The third step is to develop in foresight the consequences of your proposals. . . . The fourth and final step in thinking is to compare the consequences of your proposals to see which is best in the light of your scheme of life as a whole. . . . Whether you choose a vacation or a spouse, a party or a candidate, a cause to contribute to or a creed to live by—think!
                    —Brand Blanchard

Productivity

[*Establish a relationship*] *in which it is o.k. for everybody to do their best*. There are an awful lot of people in management who really don't want subordinates to do their best, because it gets to be very threatening. But we have found that both internally and with outside designers if we are willing to have this kind of relationship and if we're willing to be vulnerable to what will come out of it, we get really good work.
—Max De Pree

The way to get higher productivity is to train better managers and have fewer of them.
—William Woodside

I believe there is a direct relationship between people's feelings and their productivity. Innovation occurs when people feel involved and stimulated and have a sense of loyalty and commitment. . . . If the corporation doesn't give, it doesn't get. For both the individual and collective good, then, we must change the corporate code; we must build in breathing room and create opportunities for people to blow off some steam. Perhaps those in the corner offices would do well to listen to the advice of one of history's most creative thinkers expressed in these lines written for the Duke of Albany in *King Lear:*

> The weight of this sad time we must obey.
> Speak what we feel,
> Not what we ought to say.
> —Abraham Zaleznik

The key to success in business is understanding of the world about you and then making products to fit the needs of the times. A person who looks inward is bound to try to make the times try to fit his company's products.
—Pieter C. Vink

(*See* Excellence, People-Centering.)

Proficiency

Know, all the good that individuals find,
Or God and Nature meant to mere Mankind,
Reason's whole pleasure, all the joys of Sense,
Lie in three words, Health, Peace, and Competence.
                    —Alexander Pope

Guard against the temptation to argue directly from skill to capacity, and to assume when a man displays skill in some feat, his capacity is therefore considerable.
                    —Tom H. Pear

(*See* Capabilities.)

Profit and Loss

When people leave us today to become entrepreneurs, I advise them, when they say their prayers at night, to pray about their P. & L. statement. If your P. & L. is not so simple you can remember every line, or if it's not yours and not in your heart, you don't know what you want and you don't know what your plans are.
                    —Kenneth H. Olsen

(*See* Entrepreneurial Spirit, Starting a Business, Venturing.)

Progress

You can't sit on the lid of progress. If you do, you will be blown
to pieces.
                    —Henry J. Kaiser

Be not afraid of going slowly, be only afraid of standing still.
                    —Chinese proverb

(*See* Action.)

Promises

We ought not to raise expectations which it is not in our power to
satisfy. It is more pleasing to see smoke brightening into flame,
than flame sinking into smoke.
                    —Samuel Johnson

Never promise more than you can perform.
                    —Publilius Syrus

Magnificent promises are always to be suspected.
                    —Theodore Parker

The best way to keep one's word is not to give it.
                    —Napoleon I

Prosperity

Should your riches increase, let your mind keep pace with them.
                    —Sir Thomas Browne

Command your wealth, else it will command you.
—English proverb

Use your prosperity with so much caution and prudence as may not suffer you to forget yourself, or despise your inferior.
—George Shelley

(*See* Making Money.)

Proximity

Stand not too near the rich man lest he destroy thee—and not too far away lest he forget thee.
—Aneurin Bevan

Prudence

Never renew an attack along the same line or in the same form once it has been beaten back.
—David J. Rogers

We should on all occasions avoid a general Action, or put anything to Risque, unless compelled by a necessity, into which we ought never to be drawn.
—George Washington to the President of Congress

Make no deals in my name.
—Abraham Lincoln
Wire sent to 1860 Republican Convention

In your friendships, and in your enmities, let your confidence, and your hostilities have certain bounds; make not the former dangerous, nor the latter irreconcilable. There are strange vicissitudes in business!
> —Lord Chesterfield

Beware the big play: the 80-yard drive is better than the 80-yard pass.
> —Fran Tarkenton

(See Boldness, Risk.)

Public Relations

Designate a single spokesman for the company. This should not be you. You need a professional to deal with professionals.
> —Robert L. Woodrum

If you're ever right, never let them forget it.
> —Edgar Fiedler

Management principles: Tell the truth. Prove it with actions. Listen to the consumer. Manage for tomorrow. Conduct public relations as if the whole company depends on it.
> —Arthur H. Page

(See Image, Media, Press Conferences.)

Public Service

Do not separate yourself from the community.
> —Hillel

Never regret the time that was needed for doing good.
                    —Joseph Joubert

(*See* Corporate Giving, Philanthropy.)

Purpose

Pursue one great decisive aim with force and determination.
                    —Karl von Clausewitz
                    Principles of War, 1812 (Clausewitz
                    called this "a maxim which should take
                    first place among all causes of
                    victory.")

At the top there are great simplifications. An accepted leader has only to be sure of what is best to do, or at least have his mind made up about it.
                    —Winston Churchill

(*See* Determination, Resolution, Self-Direction.)

Q

Quality Control

Be a yardstick of quality. Some people aren't used to an environment where excellence is expected.
>> —Stephen Jobs

This is what every young man in business should know: that absolutely nothing is good enough if it can be made better, and better is never good enough if it can be made best.
>> —Edward W. Bok

Serve the customer. You have to have your costs right, quality right, all those other things that have to be done. But we must always think the customer is the middle of the thrust of what we are trying to do.
>> —Edson P. Williams

Never lose sight of the fact that we are here to serve the customer. If we don't serve the customer well, another retailer will.
>> —Robert Gill

In the increasing demand for quality, the consumer is about to get a powerful new tool: computer software programs to evaluate the

189

quality of goods and services. . . . We may be moving toward a truly consumer-ruled economy. Let the seller beware.
—John Naisbitt and Patricia Aburdene

Beware: The first time you still knowingly ship "slightly substandard" goods to the customer, because of tight deadlines or other pressures, your credibility at the grass roots is gone. "They don't really mean it upstairs, they're just talking." Which is your culture?
—Michael J. Kami

Questionable Advice

Do not have business transactions where there is friendship; if you have business transactions, do not lend; if you do lend, forget it.
—Punjabi proverb

Don't go in the office expecting it to be a good day. Then you'll be surprised if it is.
—Joe Paterno

You can never have riches in great quantities unless you can work yourself into a white heat of *desire* for money.
—Napoleon Hill

Avoid saying "hello." This elsewhere pleasant and familiar greeting is out of place in the world of business.
—Morgan Guaranty Trust
Instruction to its employees

Surround yourself with the best people you can find, delegate authority, and don't interfere as long as the policy you've decided upon is being carried out.
—Ronald Reagan

A prince must imitate the fox and the lion, for the lion cannot protect himself from traps, and the fox cannot defend himself from

wolves . . . a prudent ruler ought not to keep faith when by so doing it would be against his interest.
                    —Niccolò Machiavelli

If a guy works for you, don't let him get too comfortable. Don't let him get cozy or set in his ways. Always do the opposite of what he expects. Keep your people anxious and off-balance.
                    —Attributed to Henry Ford II by Lee J.
                    Iacocca

A man who has to be convinced to act before he acts is *not* a man of action. You must act as you breathe.
                    —Georges Clemenceau

At all but the highest levels of the chemical and textile industries, the rules for making gut decisions are, in the words of one upper middle manager: "(1) Avoid making any decisions if at all possible; and (2) if a decision has to be made, involve as many people as you can so that, if things go south, you're able to point in as many directions as possible."
                    —Robert Jackall

If you want to run a business—ask a man who doesn't have any.
                    —Joey Adams

In the discharge of the duties of the office, there is one rule of action more important than all others. It consists in never doing anything that someone else can do for you.
                    —Calvin Coolidge

The man who makes an appearance in the business world, the man who creates personal interest, is the man who gets ahead. Be liked and you will never want.
                    —Willy Loman, in Arthur Miller's *Death
                    of a Salesman*

Obey the spur of the moment. . . . Let the spurs of countless moments goad us incessantly into life.
                    —Henry David Thoreau

Quitting

Don't confuse what's good for you and what's good for the company. . . . If your reasons conflict with your firm's objectives, you've got a problem . . . either your values must change or the job should. Beware if you're frequently arranging your values to align them with those objectives; you may be learning how to do business in an unfamiliar environment, but you may also be prostituting yourself. You can't be happy if you've surrendered your dignity. That's when it's time to get out.
—Peter A. Reinhardt

There's a trick to the Graceful Exit. It begins with the vision to recognize when a job, a life stage, a relationship is over—and let it go. It means leaving what's over without denying its validity or its past importance to our lives. It involves a sense of future, a belief that every exit line is an entry, that we are moving on, rather than out.
—Ellen Goodman

Don't compete when you can't—get out and, unless circumstances change profoundly, stay out.
—Robert Heller

Tempted as you may be to walk off in a huff, *don't*. Leaving your job can be a chance to begin a new—and profitable—relationship with your former boss.
—*Success* magazine

First, make sure you give plenty of notice. If you've treated your boss fairly, you can expect an awful lot of help.
—Diane Holloway

Don't burn your bridges.
—James C. Cabrera

(*See* Retirement.)

R

Raiding

I'm amused when other agencies try to hire my people away.
They'd have to "hire" the whole environment. For a flower to
blossom, you need the right soil as well as the right seed.
—William Bernbach

Raises

When you give a guy a raise, that's the time to increase his responsibilities. While he's in a good frame of mind, you reward him
for what he's done, and at the same time, you motivate him to do
even more. Always hit him with more while he's up, and never be
too hard on him when he's down.
—Lee J. Iacocca

Discern what your boss wants in return for a raise or promotion.
Establish your walkaway point—and stick to it.
—Robert Bell

Withhold not good from them to whom it is due, when it is in the
power of thine hand to do it.
                    —Proverbs 3:27

Rashness

Decide not rashly. The decision made
Can never be recalled. The gods implore not,
Plead not, solicit not; they only offer
Choice and occasion, which once being passed
Return no more. Dost thou accept the gift?
                    —Henry Wadsworth Longfellow

Beware of rashness, but with energy and sleepless vigilance go
forward and give us victories.
                    —Abraham Lincoln
                    Letter to General Joseph Hooker

(*See* Impetuousness, Risk.)

Reaching for the Moon

Never apply for what you see very little probability of obtaining;
for you will, by asking improper and unattainable things, accustom
the Ministers to refuse you so often, that they will find it easy to
refuse the properest, and most reasonable ones.
                    —Lord Chesterfield

Reciprocity

One hand washes the other; give and take.
>—Epicharmus (6th–5th cent. B.C.)

Recreation

The great secret of success is to go through life as a man who never gets used up.
>—Albert Schweitzer

>Our minds need relaxations and give way
>Unless we mix work and a little play.
>—Molière

Refresh that part of thyself which is most wearied. If thy life is sedentary, exercise the body; if stirring and active, recreate thy mind.
>—Thomas Fuller

Everything which is properly *business* we must keep carefully separate from life. Business requires earnestness and method; life must have a freer handling.
>—Goethe

(*See* Executive Health, Family Values, Fun, Workaholism.)

Recruiting

Bring me men to match my mountains,
Bring me men to match my plains,
Men with empires in their purpose,
And new eras in their brains.
                    —Sam Walter Foss

Be good or begone.
                    —Bear Bryant

No matter how good or successful you are or how clever or crafty, your business and its future are in the hands of the people you hire. To put it a bit more dramatically, the fate of your business is actually in the hands of the youngest recruit on the staff. That is why I make it a point personally to address all our incoming college graduates each year.
                    —Akio Morita

I say what we need in this campaign is a Charlie Grimm. I say that because once, when Charlie was managing the Chicago Cubs, who were (need I say it?) losing, he got a phone call from one of his scouts. The man was excited and began to shout over the telephone.

"Charlie, I've landed the greatest young pitcher in the land. He struck out every man who came to bat. Twenty-seven in a row. Nobody even got a foul until two were out in the ninth. The pitcher is right here with me. What shall I do?"

Said Charlie, "Sign up the guy who got the foul. We're looking for hitters."
                    —Linda Ellerbee

Recruitment (Leadership Potential)

Do you have any junior leaders in your organization? Reward them by sending them to work with your best people and they will reward you with more leaders. . . . Growing leadership talent is not a black art and does not require the services of industrial witch doctors.

—Jack Falvey

(*See* Evaluation, Hiring.)

Red Tape

I give orders only when they are necessary. I expect them to be executed at once and to the letter and that no unit under my command shall make changes, still less give orders to the contrary or delay execution through unnecessary red tape.

—Field Marshal Erwin Rommel

Cutting red tape must become a major objective. . . . In times of faster change, faster distribution, faster saturation, and faster obsolescence, bureaucratic red tape must give way to simplification and common sense.

—Michael J. Kami

(*See* Bureaucracy.)

Reorganization

When it is not necessary to change, it is necessary not to change.
                    —Lucius Cary (Viscount Falkland)

Don't ever take a fence down until you know the reason why it was put up.
                    —Gilbert Keith Chesterton

(*See* Restructuring, Turnarounds.)

Repetition

The way to make a fortune is to sell a necessity that is low in cost and repeats. The fortune is made in the repeat business.
                    —W. Clement Stone

Buy something people use once and throw away.
                    —Attributed to Bernard M. Baruch

Reprimand

Remember, before you reprimand someone, make sure you have the facts and see that there are no extenuating circumstances. Sometimes a decline in performance is caused by a drop in confidence—the job is more complicated than anticipated. When that happens, you don't reprimand; you provide support and encouragement, and if necessary, direction.
                    —Kenneth Blanchard, Patricia Zigarmi,
                    Drea Zigarmi

Never rebuke a man in such a way as to shame him in public.
—Rashi

You may scold a carpenter who has made you a bad table, though you cannot make a table. It is not your trade to make tables.
—Samuel Johnson

There is a time to wink as well as to see.
—American proverb

Rebuke not in anger, or with severity; hard words are like hailstones in summer, beating down and destroying what they would nourish were they melted into drops.
—Tryon Edwards

Never give a man a dollar's worth of blame without a dime's worth of praise.
—Colonel L. P. Hunt, USMC

(*See* Criticism, Praise.)

Reputation

Never risk your reputation on a single shot for if you miss, the loss is irreparable. . . . Always hold in reserve recourse to something better, and the reputation of having something more.
—Baltasar Gracián

There are men in the world, who to advance their own fame, will descry the virtue and merit of other people. Never think of raising your reputation by detraction.
—W. de Britaine

Let not the covetous design of growing rich induce you to ruin your reputation, but rather satisfy yourself with a moderate fortune;

and let your thoughts be wholly taken up with acquiring to yourself
a glorious name.
                                                    —John Dryden

Beware of the man that has no regard to his own reputation, since
it is not likely he should have any for yours.
                                                    —George Shelley

Envy we must overcome by generosity and nobleness of soul;
anger, by a repos'd and easy mind; riot and drowsiness, by vigilance
and temperance; lasciviousness, by our inviolable fidelity to those
who are mistresses of our thoughts; and sloth, by our indefatigable
peregrinations through the universe. . . . This, Sancho, is the road
to lasting fame, and a good and honourable renown.
                                                    —Cervantes

Reserve

The great secret of battle is to have a reserve. I always had.
                                    —Arthur Wellesley, Duke of Wellington

Fatigue the opponent, if possible, with few forces and conserve a
decisive mass for the critical moment. Once this decisive mass has
been thrown in, it must be used with the greatest audacity.
                                                    —Karl von Clausewitz

(*See* Preparation.)

Research and Development

There's a way to do it better—Find it.
>   —Thomas A. Edison to a research
>   associate

(*See* New Ideas.)

Resolution

> Be as a tower, firmly set
> Shakes not its top for any blast that
> blows.
>   —Dante

Respect for Authority

Another thing that a lot of management experts advocate importing from the Far East is that the boss should be one of the boys. Democratic as that philosophy may sound, I don't think it's very practical. If the boss lets his hair down too much, he ends up like Rodney Dangerfield. No respect.
>   —Lee J. Iacocca

Respect for the Individual

In real life, the most practical advice for leaders is not to treat pawns like pawns, nor princes like princes, but all persons like *persons*.

—James MacGregor Burns

(*See* People-Centering.)

Responsibility

The first responsibility of a leader is to define reality. The last is to say thank you. In between the two, the leader must become a servant and a debtor. . . . A friend of mine characterized leaders simply like this: "Leaders don't inflict pain; they bear pain."

—Max De Pree

Restraint

Be not angry that you cannot make others as you wish them to be, since you cannot make yourself as you wish to be.

—Thomas à Kempis

You must never be satisfied with losing. You must get angry, terribly angry, about losing. But the mark of the good loser is that he *takes his anger out on himself* and not on his victorious opponents or on his teammates.

—Richard Nixon, after losing presidential
election in 1960

Eat within your stomach, act within your commission.
— John Selden, 1666

(*See* Self-Control.)

Restructuring

When you build your castle, and you build it to be strong and good
and what you want, never be afraid to bring it down and make it
flat, if that's what you have to do to go ahead with life. You have
to get your emotions out of it.
— Emanuel Fthenakis (paraphrase of
Greek poem)

Whether CEO's like it or not, capital markets now demand that
they monitor the "value gap" between what the company's shareholders realize now and what they might be able to get. . . . The
solution: CEO's must start thinking and acting like raiders themselves. First, they need to assess their companies' situations—
measure the value gap and track it periodically. . . . CEO's can
choose one or more of three basic options: improve operations,
leverage the company's capital structure, or sell business units to
the "best buyers." . . . Executives can also throw legal hurdles—
like poison pills or dual class shares with different voting rights—
in the path of potential acquirers.
— William E. Fruhan, Jr.

(*See* also Leveraged Buyouts, Reorganization, Takeovers,
Turnarounds.)

Retaliation

Man must evolve for all human conflict a method which rejects revenge, aggression and retaliation. The foundation of such a method is love.
>   —Martin Luther King, Jr.

The only way to secure future ease is to take up a proper position early in life, and show that you will not be insulted with impunity.
>   —Benjamin Disraeli

Don't go looking for a fight—but if you're hit, *deck* the bastard.
>   —Roger Ailes

Repudiate the repudiators!
>   —Wm. P. Fessenden
>   Presidential Canvass of 1868

Attacks must be answered. An assertion unanswered is an assertion agreed to.
>   —Geoff Garin

Never get into a spraying match with a skunk.
>   —Mark Hatfield

Forget living well. The best revenge is revenge.
>   —William Hamilton
>   Cartoon caption in *The New Yorker*

Retiring

Leave the court before the court leave thee. The well timing of a retreat is the glory of it, and shows the foresight and conduct of a

general. If some of the greatest men had understood the just season to retire, it had saved them their honor and their life too.
— Samuel Palmer

When you are no longer fit to hold a position, do not be tempted by avarice or pride to continue in it but retire when your energies are still active. When meritorious services have led to fame it is time to follow the heavenly rule and to retire into obscurity.
— Lao-tzu

There is a time to stay and a time to go. You tip your hat when you're on top, and say goodbye. There's no greater tragedy for a person of ability, character and prestige than to try to stay that one extra term. You forget that you don't have a lock on anything forever. . . . Once you are out of office, don't try to second guess. Be an observer, not a participant. Forget the power that you had. Be available for advice and friendship, but don't try to run the show any more.
— Abraham Ribicoff

An abrupt stop is a great mistake. I think it's wise to keep your hand on the plough. If you have quit your job, find something like it to do part-time or find substitute activities, such as volunteer work or getting involved in politics. Or join a group that deals with problems of aging or some other cause that interests you. Keep busy; stay involved.
— B. F. Skinner

(*See* Quitting.)

Risk

First reckon, then risk.
— Helmuth von Moltke ("the Elder")

If I find the French convoy in any place where there is a probability of attacking them, you may depend they shall either be taken or

destroyed at the risk of my squadron . . . which is built to be risked on proper occasions.
                                   —Admiral Horatio Nelson

If you miss seven balls out of ten, you're batting three hundred, and that's good enough for the Hall of Fame. You can't score if you keep the bat on your shoulder.
                                   —Walter B. Wriston

(*See* Boldness, Prudence.)

Rules

Challenge the rules. Inspect your own rules. Fall out of love with your own rules and ideas. Think frivolously. Make jokes about the problem you are working on.
                                   —Roger Von Oech

S

Salesmanship

Give the lady what she wants.
— Marshall Field's department store
motto

Be everywhere, do everything and never fail to astonish the customer.
— Macy's motto

Sam [Walton, founder of Wal-Mart] asks the associates to raise their right hands and execute a pledge, keeping in mind that "a promise we make is a promise we keep." The pledge: "From this day forward, I solemnly promise and declare that every customer that comes within ten feet of me, I will smile at, look them in the eye, and greet them, so help me Sam." You city slicker CEOs laugh all you want. This is one of the keys to the magic formula.
— John Huey

Saving

Saving

There is one sure mark of the coming partner, the future millionaire; his revenues always exceed his expenditures. He begins to save early, almost as soon as he starts to earn. . . . Gentlemen, it is the first hundred dollars saved which tells. Begin at once to lay up something.
—Andrew Carnegie

If you would be wealthy, think of saving as well as getting.
—Benjamin Franklin

Secrets

You must not kiss and tell.
—William Congreve

Security Analysts

Always, always—never talk about what you're going to do, and don't tell them what you're not going to do.
—Richard Nixon

Self-Control

Be swift to hear, slow to speak, slow to wrath.
—James 1:19

Never suffer your courage to exert itself in fierceness, your resolution in obstinacy, your wisdom in cunning, nor your patience in sullenness and despair.
—Charles Palmer

(*See* Restraint.)

Self-Direction

Consider well who you are, what you do, whence you came, and whither you are to go.
—English proverb

(*See* Purpose.)

Self-Esteem

A man had better overvalue than undervalue himself. Mankind in general will take his own word for his own merit.

. . . know your own value, whatever it may be, and act upon that principle; but take great care to let nobody discover that you do know your own value. Whatever real merit you have, other people will discover; and people always magnify their own discoveries, as they lessen those of others.
—Lord Chesterfield

Never wish to exchange your troubles for those of another.
—Jacqueline Markham's mother

(*See* Confidence.)

Self-Promotion

Worry not that no one knows of you; seek to be worth knowing.
                    —Confucius

Selling Companies

If you have something that doesn't fit with your operations, sell it.
Don't try to get top dollar for it. You more than make up for any
difference you might get by being able to concentrate on the business you should be concentrating on.
                    —Sanford I. Weill

(*See* Takeovers.)

Sex

Hugging, kissing or cornering female employees is almost always
inappropriate. Friendly touching, such as a pat on the back or an
arm around the shoulder, is a little trickier and depends largely
on your relationship with the employee. To play it absolutely safe,
any form of touching beyond a handshake should be avoided if you
are in a power position.
                    —Stephen Andersen

Keep in mind that you are a role model to your subordinates,
including your secretary. . . . The extension of anti-discrimination
laws to cover "sexual harassment" now adds a legal as well as moral
deterrent to taking advantage of one's position as an employer.
Such misconduct is defined by the Equal Employment Opportun-

ities Commission to "include unwelcome sexual advances, requests for sexual favors and other verbal or physical conduct of a sexual nature." The term "verbal conduct" covers unwelcome off-color or suggestive remarks. . . . Aware that such prohibitions exist, the executive must be sure to draw a line between coarseness and humor.

> —Mortimer R. Feinberg and Aaron
> Levenstein

(*See* Office Romance.)

Shading the Truth

So near is falsehood to truth that a wise man would do well not to trust himself on the narrow edge.
> —Cicero

You have the right to remain silent, but you can never, repeat, never lie or shade the truth.
> —Robert L. Woodrum

When greeted upon his return to power by cries of "Algérie Fran-çaise!" [De Gaulle] answered his countrymen, "Je vous ai compris" ("I have understood you"). Indeed he had. But he did not say he would keep Algeria French. No leader can lie, or condone official lying, without turning totalitarian. But he may, and often must, tell what one political scientist calls "the truth, the partial truth, and nothing but the truth."
> —Brock Brower

(*See* Honesty, Truth in Advertising.)

Socializing

Although all words of command should be given in an authoritative and firm tone, it does not follow that drill manners should accompany the officer into private society.
—Colonel J. G. D. Tucker

The commander must try, above all, to establish personal and comradely contact with his men, but without giving away an inch of his authority.

—Field Marshal Erwin Rommel

Speculation

Don't speculate unless you make it your life's work. Amateurs always go broke.
Never play tips from "insiders." They can't see the forest for the trees.
Keep a strong cash reserve and never trade on margins.
—Bernard M. Baruch

Baruch made his pile as a speculator. . . . He added that the word derives from the latin "speculor, speculari: to observe. I observe, gentlemen, I observe." . . . The only wisdom he brought to the Crash was his maxim about running for cover—"Run quickly"— which he luckily observed.
—*Fortune* magazine

Buy when everyone is selling. And hold until everyone is buying.
—J. Paul Getty

Keep emotion out of your stock decision-making process. Love your spouse, your children, but don't love your stocks. Just because

they have been good to you in the past is no guarantee they will
be good to you in the future.
                    —Anne E. Brown

Buy land; they are not making it anymore.
                    —Mark Twain

Buy on the rumor. Sell on the news.
                    —Wall Street adage

(*See* Investing.)

Speechmaking

You *must* know your audience. If you're not already an insider,
find out everything there is to know about the group, and tailor
your remarks accordingly. If that's not worth doing, the speech
isn't worth giving.
                    —Ed Wohlmuth

You do not need to shout if you use the right words.
                    —Anon.

If your diction is slipshod and impure, correct and purify it; don't
throw it away and make shift for the rest of your life with a hideous
affectation accent, false emphases, unmeaning pauses, aggravating
slowness, ill-conditioned gravity, and perverse resolution to "get
it from the chest" and make it sound as if you got it from the cellar.
                    —George Bernard Shaw

Never exaggerate. . . . Exaggeration is akin to lying; and through
it you jeopardize your reputation for good taste, which is much,
and for good judgment, which is more.
                    —Baltasar Gracián

Be guided by the speaker who preceded you. If he finished with
a laugh, you should start seriously—and the other way around.

. . . To get a laugh, for example, I may say, "Ladies and gentlemen, before I begin my address, I have something to say."
                    —George Jessel

Speak not with a stiff neck.
                    —Psalms 75:5

Try not to beat back the current, yet be not drowned in the waters; speak with the speech of the world, think with the thoughts of the few.
                    —John Hay

Think today, and speak tomorrow.
                    —H. C. Bohn

One thing a speaker should remember for sure;
The mind can absorb only what the seat can endure.
                    —Maxwell Droke

The ideal speech is about 20 minutes. You can always tell when you've talked too long. People start rattling their coffee cups or fiddling around with their dessert.
                    —Robert Orben

Because the element of surprise is basic to provoking laughter, do not alert your audience to the idea that a joke is coming, "which reminds me of a story." If you have a quip based on current headlines, make sure that many in your audience have read the same newspapers that you have. Before delivering any humorous remark, double-check it for sexism, racism, and personal antagonism or lack of feeling toward lower-echelon employees. After the laughter fades, the audience may resent your display of power.
                    —Business Week

You don't lead people by following them, but by saying what they want to follow.
                    —Enoch Powell

To make others feel we must feel ourselves; and to feel ourselves we must be natural.
                    —Benjamin Disraeli

Take eloquence and wring its neck!
> —Paul Verlaine

Don't take any wooden rhetoric!
> —S. J. Perelman

> Boys flying kites haul in their white-winged birds;
> You can't do that way when you're flying words.
> "Careful with fire" is good advice, we know;
> "Careful with words" is ten times double so.
> Thoughts unexpressed may sometimes fall back dead;
> But God himself can't kill them when they're said.
> > —Poem often quoted by Warren
> > Harding

Don't be so loud all the time as to make it impossible to raise the voice to drive home a point.
> —Strom Thurmond

Standards

I'd push people back to their typewriters and drawing tables, telling them: "You *can* do better; you *have* to do better." And they'd do better. Good people respond to high standards.
> —Shepard Kurnit

(*See* Example, Excellence.)

Starting a Business

Before you launch any business, take a hard look at its real market potential. Do not try to start too big. The safest course is to create a firm small enough for the money you have and then make it larger. A small success is better than a big failure. Be sure you start with enough money. Underfinancing is as bad as overborrowing. It can choke a promising enterprise or force you to give up control to your backers. A little financial help from your friends and relatives is fine, but treat such loans as strictly business deals, complete with signed legal agreements. Handshake deals often lead to bitter quarrels.

—Marshall Loeb

Whatever you think it's gonna take, double it. That applies to money, time, stress. It's gonna be harder than you think and take longer than you think.

—Richard A. Cortese

Don't overrun your funds and jeopardize your strategy. Don't undercapitalize your company, and *never* take on a underfunded strategy with hopes that it will somehow work out.

—Roy Ash

Research your market, but do not take too long to act.
Start your business when you have a customer.
Try your new venture as a sideline at first.
Plan your objectives within specific time frames.
Surround yourself with people who are smarter than yourself—
   including an outside board of directors.
Don't be afraid to fail.
Hire a great accountant.

—John Naisbitt and Patricia Aburdene

Never acquire a business you don't know how to run.

—Robert W. Johnson

Your confidence in a product or venture must be strong. If your feelings are lukewarm, you need more information before deciding the extent of your involvement. . . . The lesson is simple: You can't sell anything that you wouldn't buy yourself.

—Victor Kiam

(*See* Entrepreneurial Spirit, Profit and Loss, Venturing.)

Strategic Planning (Long-Range Planning)

When any great design thou dost intend
Think on the means, the manner and the end.
—John Dunham

In action, be primitive; in foresight, a strategist.
—René Char

Strategic planning is necessary precisely because we cannot fore-cast. . . . Strategic planning does not deal with future decisions. It deals with the futurity of present decisions. Decisions exist only in the present. The question that faces the strategic decision-maker is not what his organization should do tomorrow. It is: "What do we have to do today to be ready for an uncertain tomorrow?"
—Peter F. Drucker

Let our advance worrying become advance thinking and planning.
—Winston Churchill

Steer not in every mariner's direction.
—Thomas Fuller

Never take anything for granted.
—Benjamin Disraeli

Telling people what you plan dissipates the drama of those plans when you get around to their execution and gains you nothing, since people dismiss what you are going to do for them "someday soon" as vainglory. Wait until you are ready.
—Robert J. Schoenberg

Make no needless plans.
—General Robert E. Lee

Successful generals make plans to fit circumstances, but do not try to create circumstances to fit plans.
                    —General George S. Patton, Jr.

(*See* Forecasting, Gut Feelings, Hunches, Intelligence [Industrial, Military], Planning, Preparation.)

Strength

"Draw strength from each other." There is a story that one night in 1945, General Dwight Eisenhower walked along the Rhine, thinking of the crossing in which he would lead Allied armies. He met a soldier and asked him why he wasn't sleeping. The young G.I. didn't recognize the Supreme Commander. "I guess I'm a little nervous," he said. "Well, so am I," said Eisenhower. "Let's walk together and perhaps we'll draw strength from each other."
                    —James A. Renier

The best strategy is always to be strong.
                    —Karl von Clausewitz

Know your weaknesses. Acknowledge them. But don't worry about them. As long as you understand your shortcomings, you will go out of your way to hire people with strengths to offset them.
                    —Joseph Solomon

Stress

One of my lawyers once told me to read the sports section first every morning. It talks more about mankind's successes, while other parts talk about mankind's problems or failures.
                    —Michael R. Milken

Remember, you can't make a race horse out of a turtle.
—Hans Selye

(*See* Executive Health.)

Style

Be like jockey Willie Shoemaker. He's the best in the business because he has the lightest touch on the reins. They say the horse never knows he's there—unless he's needed.
—Harvey Mackay

What style works well for one manager in a particular situation may not produce the desired results for another manager in a similar situation. . . . Every manager . . . must develop his own natural style and follow practices that are consistent with his own personality.
—J. S. Livingston

(*See* Bosses, Leadership [Personal].)

Success

If you wish success in life, make perseverance your bosom friend, experience your wise counselor, caution your elder brother and hope your guardian genius.
—Joseph Addison

The secret of success in life is for a man to be ready for his time when it comes.
—Benjamin Disraeli

Be not crushed under success, in order not to be crushed under
envy.
> —Baltasar Gracián

Honesty. Hard work. Aggressiveness. Temperance. Consideration
for others. Tried and true principles these. Tenets that have stood
the test of time—by dint of which Ragged Dick, Phil the Fiddler
and other Alger lads just might make it in today's business world.
Formulas for success just haven't changed all that much in the last
hundred years.
> —Ralph D. Gardner, member, Horatio
> Alger Society of Lansing, Michigan

Rockefeller once explained the secret of success. "Get up early,
work late—and strike oil."
> —Joey Adams

Succession

We must live by the Quick, and not by the Dead.
> —Thomas Fuller

From a management viewpoint, Shakespeare's King Lear is a tragedy because Lear failed to understand two managerial precepts:
the need to select competent successors and the need to let go.
Like many contemporary managers, he led an enterprise that
thrived for many years under his leadership. But also like many
contemporary managers, he was unable to manage the end of his
career and thus destroyed the enterprise. Leaders should remind
themselves of the words that Andrew Carnegie had inscribed on
his tombstone: "Here lies a man who knew how to enlist in his
service better men than himself."
> —John K. Clemens and Douglas F.
> Mayer

Be like an oak tree—your branches spreading out widely so that
new saplings may grow in their shade. You must not be a beech

tree, growing so straight that you give no shade to the next generation.
—Harold Macmillan

When we are planning for posterity, we ought to remember that virtue is not hereditary.
—Thomas Paine

Surprises

A true leader always keeps an element of surprise up his sleeve, which others cannot grasp but which keeps his public excited and breathless.
—Charles de Gaulle

Getting the right information is a substantial part of the job [of management]. The basic ground rule is that you can't be taken by surprise. You get lots of information and most of it is totally unnecessary. The organization tends to want to give you the good news and not cough up the bad news. But to manage well, you have to get the message across that whatever the story is, let's get it on the table fast so there are no surprises. But it doesn't always happen that way.
—Irving I. Shapiro

Surprise your antagonist. . . . Keep up the moral ascendancy which the first successful rising has given you.
—V. I. Lenin

One piece of advice to all presidents that is guaranteed: *Prepare to be surprised.*
—Stephen Hess

(*See* Deception, Intelligence [Industrial, Military], Offensive Strategy.)

Sycophants

Tzu-lu asked how to serve the King. The Master said: "Never cheat him: withstand him to the face."
   —Confucius

Watch the faces of those who bow low.
   —Polish proverb

Do not saddle yourself with fools; he is one who does not know them, and a greater, he who knowing them, does not shake them off, for they are dangerous in the daily round and deadly as confidants.
   —Baltasar Gracián

If you act like an ass, don't get insulted if people ride you.
   —Yiddish proverb

Never let your inferiors do you a favor—it will be extremely costly.
   —H. L. Mencken

(*See* Yes-Men.)

Synergism

How would you sum up the Intel approach? Many hands would go up and Grove would choose one and the communicant would say: "At Intel you don't wait for someone else to do it. You take the ball yourself and you run with it." And Grove would say: "Wrong. At Intel you take the ball yourself and you let the air out and you fold the ball up and put it in your pocket. Then you take another ball and run with it and when you've crossed the goal you take the second ball out of your pocket and reinflate it and score twelve points instead of six."

—Philosophical principles of Intel
explained by Andrew Grove

T

Tact

You must have a rare amount of patience. You must give no umbrage. You must always try to hear everything the other person says. I never knew a person who didn't become tractable if you didn't threaten him with a meat axe. The oil can is mightier than the sword.

—Everett Dirksen

To manage men, one ought to have a sharp mind in a velvet sheath.
—George Eliot

Always be tactful and well mannered and teach your subordinates to be the same. Avoid excessive sharpness or harshness of voice, which usually indicates the man who has shortcomings of his own to hide.

—Field Marshal Erwin Rommel

(*See* Diplomacy.)

Takeovers

A general-in-chief should ask himself frequently in the day, "What would I do if the enemy's army appeared now in my front, or on my right, or my left?" If he has any difficulty in answering these questions, his position is bad, and he should seek to remedy it.
—Napoleon I

How to drive off a raider:
Hit 'em with a business plan.
Don't play the other guy's game.
Get ready to go to court.
Try anything that might work.
—*Newsweek*

Once the enemy has been thoroughly beaten up, success can be exploited by attempting to overrun and destroy major parts of his disorganized formations. Here again, speed is everything. The enemy must never be allowed time to reorganize. Lightning regrouping for the pursuit and reorganization of supplies for the pursuing forces are essential.
—Field Marshal Erwin Rommel

Takeovers (Hostile)

Go into emptiness, strike voids, bypass what he defends, hit him where he does not expect you.
—Ts'ao Ts'ao (A.D. 155–220)

While invading an enemy's territory, men should always be confident in spirit, but they should fear, too, and take measures of

precaution; and thus they will be at once most valorous in attack
and impregnable in defense.

—Archidamus of Sparta

(*See* Deception, Leveraged Buyouts, Negotiating, Offensive
Strategy, Selling Companies.)

Talent

Honour talent wherever you behold it associated with vice; but
honour it most when accompanied with exertion, and especially
when exerted in the cause of truth and justice; and, above all things,
hold it in honour, when it steps forward to protect defenceless
innocence against the attacks of powerful guilt.

—William Cobbett

Teamwork

Trying to change individual and/or corporate behavior without ad-
dressing the larger organizational context is bound to disappoint.
Sooner or later bureaucratic structures will consume even the most
determined of collaborative processes. As Woody Allen once said,
"The lion and the lamb may lie down together, but the lamb won't
get much sleep." What to do? Work on the lion as well as the lamb
by designing teamwork into the organization. . . . Although the
Boston Celtics have won 16 championships, they have never had
the league's leading scorer and never paid a player based on his
individual statistics. The Celtics understand that virtually every
aspect of basketball requires close collaboration.

—Robert W. Keidel

Work Together—Even When Apart. We wanted to get away from
the idea that work was a zero-sum game. Instead of running op-

erations that created a few winners and many losers, we made it clear that our goal was for everyone—each co-worker and each client—to be a winner. Success was not a trophy awarded to three or four star players. Real success would put everyone ahead. . . . We stressed that a key part of everyone's job was a responsibility to help all the people around them to succeed. Our goal was—and still remains today—to have everyone excel both as a player and a coach. That, we believe, is real teamwork.
—David A. Teiger

(*See* Control, Empowerment, Interdependence, People-Centering, Praise, Zero-Sum Game.)

Television Appearances

Never tell someone you've seen on television how much better he or she looks in person. The only thing worse is to tell them how much better they look on television. The solution: "You look great, just like on TV."
—Barbara Walters

Never forget that television is a visual medium. The person sitting out there is a passive viewer who's going to go away with an impression of you. You might be making a brilliant argument, but what the viewer will remember is whether your necklace jangled every time you turned your head, or whether the shape of your mustache made you look like a shifty character.
—Herb Schmertz

(*See* Image, Media, Press Conferences, Public Relations.)

Testing

Test your premise. Test your media. Test your headlines and your illustrations. Test your level of expenditure. Test your commercials. Never stop testing and your advertising will never stop improving.
> —Thomas J. Peters and Robert H. Waterman, Jr.

Steinbach's Guideline for Systems Programming: Never test for an error condition you don't know how to handle.
> —Arthur Bloch

Test yourself on humanity. It makes the doubtful doubt, the believer believe.
> —Franz Kafka

(*See* Market Research.)

Thinking

Never perish a good thought.
> —Malcolm Forbes

THINK. It's the one word motto of the most imitated company in the country, IBM. Don't stifle it. Encourage it.
> —Harvey Mackay

Never try to discourage thinking, for you are sure to succeed.
> —Bertrand Russell

Threats

Don't threaten. I know it's done by some of our people, but I don't go for it. If people are running scared, they're not going to make the right decisions. They'll make decisions to please the boss rather than recommend what has to be done.
—Charles Pilliod

There's a great hesitancy to tell a guy, "You're not doing the job" or "You're mediocre." But doing that is a key element in motivating them. We need to tell people, no matter how high or low, to what degree they are or aren't doing the job. You've got to come right out and tell them, "You're perceived as marginal; now you have the opportunity, and we think the capability, to do a hell of a lot better."
—Robert Baker

Never shake your fist and then shake your finger.
—Theodore Roosevelt

(*See* Motivation.)

Timidity

Be nice, feel guilty, and play safe. If there was ever a prescription for producing a dismal future, that has to be it.
—Walter B. Wriston

You cannot afford to be a carp in a pond where there are pike about.
—Otto von Bismarck

The moment a leader shows timidity he encourages people to go after him. People can sense when a leader is timid and they au-

tomatically attack. . . . Try to be conciliatory when others are conciliatory toward you, but when the other side doesn't want to heal
wounds, fight 'em—you get more respect.
                                    —Richard Nixon

(*See* Boldness, Courage, Prudence.)

Timing

You win battles . . . by knowing the enemies' timing, and thus
using a timing which the enemy does not expect.
                                    —Miyamoto Musashi

Set not your loaf in till the oven's hot.
                                    —English proverb

Listen to me, Esther, a career is a curious thing. Talent isn't always
enough. You need a sense of timing—an eye for seeing the turning
point, for recognizing the big chance when it comes along and
grabbing it. A career can rest on a trifle like—like us sitting here
tonight. Or it can turn on somebody saying to you, "You're better
than that. You're better than you know." Don't settle for the little
dream. Go on to the big one.
                                    —James Mason to Judy Garland in
                                    A Star Is Born

Take hold of a good Minute.
                                    —Thomas Fuller

In a boxing match, you can lose the first 14 rounds. All you have
to do is nail your opponent in the last 10 seconds of the 15th round
and you're the world's heavyweight champion.
                                    —H. Ross Perot

One who would grow rich must buy of those who go to be executed, as not caring how cheap they sell; and sell to those who go to be married, as not caring how dear they buy.
—Thomas Fuller

Titles

Find ways to share authority without fully relinquishing control. Leadership can be even more important when it operates within limits. All signs point to a move away from rigidly structured, hierarchical organizations in which titles and positions carry their own authority.
—Arnold Brown and Edith Weiner

Titles should never be used as rewards, let alone to cover up lack of function. Titles "in lieu of a raise" are not nearly as bad, nor as common as titles "in lieu of a job."
—Peter F. Drucker

Tough-Mindedness

No one wants to follow a weak leader. He is the worst kind. You cannot rely on his judgment because you don't know what he will do in a difficult situation. Much more respect and loyalty are given to the tough leader, the one who is not afraid to make difficult and even unpopular decisions, just as long as he is perceived to be decent and fair and reliable in his dealings with his subordinates.
—Harold Geneen

The shell is America's most active contribution to the formation of character. A tough hide. Grow it early.
—Anaïs Nin

I told them I knew they had been making trouble for the previous commanders. I said: "I didn't come over here to get along with you. You've got to get along with me. And if there are any of you who can't, speak up and I'll bust you right back." We got along.
>—Captain Harry S. Truman
>On taking command of a field artillery battalion, 1918

(*See* Command, Obedience.)

Tradition

Never throw away hastily any old faith, tradition or convention. They may require modification, but they are the result of the experience of many generations.
>—Oliver Lodge

Open the windows, let in the year we're living in.
>—Kitty D'Alessio
>On conflict between tradition and modernity, after she succeeded company founder Coco Chanel

Travel

Never be flippantly rude to elderly strangers in foreign hotels. They always turn out to be the King of Sweden.
>—"Saki" (H. H. Munro)

Those who observe, and inquire into the situations, the strength, the weakness, the trade, the manufactures, the government, and constitution of every place they go to; who frequent the best companies, and attend to their several manners and characters; those alone travel with advantage; and as they set out wise, return wiser.*
                                                    —Lord Chesterfield

*Dr. Johnson said: "As the Spanish proverb says, 'He who would bring home the wealth of the Indies must carry the wealth of the Indies with him.' So it is in travelling; a man must carry knowledge with him, if he would bring home knowledge."—Boswell's *Life of Johnson*, iii, 302.

Although handshakes are becoming more common [in Japan], especially when greeting a Westerner, traditional bows are still the rule. Bows are used for greetings and farewells, for expressing appreciation, for making apologies, and for making requests. Before and after a negotiating session, both parties will bow at least once. . . . If you would like to shake hands, you can initiate this immediately after the bow. It's something the Japanese may now expect. Since it is not a traditional part of their culture, however, it would be unwise to judge a Japanese on the firmness of his handshake in the way we might do in the West. A weak handshake may simply be from lack of practice.
                                                    —Diana Rowland

Never give a Hindu a gift made of cowhide, since the cow is considered sacred in the country of India. . . . Don't give a Britisher a striped tie. An Englishman wears only his own regiment's tie; to wear another would be considered very bad form. . . . Do not bring an Arab liquor or wine. . . . Never give a clock to the Chinese, since it is a symbol of death.
                                                    —Letitia Baldrige

(*See* Gifts [Corporate].)

Truth in Advertising

Make every bargain clear and plain
That none may afterward
complain.
         —John Ray proverb

Remember then, as long as you live, that nothing but strict truth can carry you through the world, with either your conscience or your honor unwounded. It is not only your duty, but your interest, as a proof of which, you may always observe, that the greatest fools are the greatest liars.
         —Lord Chesterfield

Invent not a lie, to get profit thereby.
         —English saying

If your philosophy is to sell anything to anybody anytime, you're inevitably going to end up selling customers who don't have a clearly defined need for your product. When that happens you Win but they Lose. You can get away with this once in a while, but eventually a customer that you trick into buying is going to find out. When he does, you can forget about repeat business, referrals, new leads—in other words, you can forget about everything that's keeping you in business.
         —Robert Miller

(*See* Advertising, Honesty.)

Turnarounds

If you are brought in to shake up a company, start mixing and matching as fast as you can. To establish credibility as a leader, do at least three of the following as soon as possible:
1. Add a new division.
2. Consolidate or lop off a present department.
3. Add new people; reassign and reward present employees.
4. Get rid of the unfireables—the people who couldn't (but should) have been fired under previous management.
5. Change the method of accounting.
   —Lois Wyse

To turn a loser into a winner you must get some answers that come best, maybe only, from competent people who have lived through the problems. So you would not want to fire everyone and start fresh even if management let you.
   —William Roesch

Executive jets, fancy lunches and stretch limos may be OK when things are going well, but they are death to a successful turnaround. Savvy turnaround managers eradicate them just as Lycurgus did.* He started by closing the board room. He had his advisers meet instead outside, rain or shine. Plutarch wrote: "Lycurgus was of the opinion that ornaments were so far from advantaging them in their councils, that they were rather a hindrance, by diverting attention from the business before them."
   —John K. Clemens

*Lycurgus was one of the leaders of Sparta, which defeated the Athenians in the Peloponnesian War.

(*See* Reorganization, Restructuring.)

U

Understanding

Leadership, like everything else in life that is vital, finds its source in understanding. To be worthy of management responsibility today, a man must have insight into the human heart, for unless he has an awareness of human problems, a sensitivity towards the hopes and aspirations of those whom he supervises, and a capacity for analysis of the emotional forces that motivate their conduct, the projects entrusted to him will not get ahead no matter how often wages are raised.

—Clarence Randall

The longer I live, and the more I attend conferences . . . the less importance I come to attach to what you might call legislation and formal resolutions, and the more importance I come to attach to what I call *atmosphere*. We want an atmosphere of understanding. If we understand each other we find it possible then to have an atmosphere of unity; to use a phrase of a speaker at the Edinburgh Conference, "An atmosphere in which men loathe to differ, and determine to understand."

—John R. Mott

(*See* Interdependence, Meetings, Morale, People-Centering.)

Unsavory Associates

You are permitted in time of great danger to walk with the devil until you have crossed the bridge.
— Bulgarian proverb

Urgency

Behave with purposeful impatience. . . . It is essential—today more than ever—not to put up with traditional excuses that come from the victory of boardroom brand civility and functional primacy over taking action.
— Tom Peters

V

Venturing

Before you join a new venture, be sure to consider certain questions: Is the new product or service really worthy? For evidence, read the founder's business plan. What is the founder's business record of past success? For information, consult his or her business associates and rivals. Who is putting up the money? A token of an entrepreneur's commitment is the amount of his or her own money invested in the new venture. The more complicated your employment arrangement, the more you will want a contract or at least a letter of understanding. Get as much down on paper as possible, then show the agreement to your lawyer.
—Marshall Loeb

Don't break your head for the sake of trying a plaster. To sin because there is forgiveness is wickedness. To indulge at table because there is medicine is folly.
—C. H. Spurgeon

Venture a small fish to catch a big one.
—John Ray proverb

(*See* Entrepreneurial Spirit, Profit and Loss, Starting a Business.)

238

Versatility

A versatility of manners is as necessary in social as a versatility of parts is in political life. One must often yield, in order to prevail; one must humble oneself, to be exalted; one must, like St. Paul, become all things to all men, to gain some.*
—Lord Chesterfield

*"I am made all things to all men, that I might by all means save some."—I Corinthians 9:22.

Victory

Pursue not a victory too far. He hath conquered well that hath made his enemy fly; thou mayest beat him to a desperate resistance, which may ruin thee.
—George Herbert

Visible Management

There are many ways to avoid mistakes, but the best way to sidestep the disasters is to be available. You don't have to make every decision, but you should always be accessible. If your people are smart they will keep you informed, and if you're informed, you're a part of the decision. With that in place, it's easy for you to back your people and it eliminates second guessing.
—T. Boone Pickens

Do not summon people to your office—it frightens them. Instead go to see them in *their* offices. This makes you visible throughout

the agency. A chairman who never wanders about his agency becomes a hermit, out of touch with his staff.
>   —David Ogilvy

>   (*See* Hands-On Managing.)

Vision

As you enter positions of trust and power, dream a little before
you think.
>   —Toni Morrison
>   Commencement address, 1988

Don't underestimate the power of a vision. McDonald's founder,
Ray Kroc, pictured his empire long before it existed, and he saw
how to get there. He invented the company motto—"Quality,
service, cleanliness and value"—and kept repeating it to employees
for the rest of his life.
>   —Kenneth Labich

The very essence of leadership is [that] you have to have a vision.
It's got to be a vision you articulate clearly and forcefully on every
occasion. You can't blow an uncertain trumpet.
>   —Theodore Hesburgh

Don't let the vision be shot through with holes, but be damned
sure some of your best and brightest are shooting at it—with ba-
zookas as well as snipers' rifles.
>   —Tom Peters

>   (*See* Goals, Higher Purpose, Long View.)

Vocational Training

Better build schoolrooms for "the boy"
Than cells and gibbets for "the man."
—Eliza Cook (1818–1889)

W

Wasting Time

No matter how well they are written . . . memos should be kept to a minimum. Any correspondence that raises an issue that can be responded to immediately should be answered by telephone. Try not to get involved in a game of dueling memos. It's wasteful.
—Victor Kiam

Don't bail a boat that does not leak. Do not try to prove a doctrine which nobody doubts, or defend that which is quite beyond attack, or vindicate a man for doing what is clearly right.
—C. H. Spurgeon

Winning/Losing

No fighter ever won his fight by covering up—by merely fending off the other's blows. The winner hits and keeps on hitting even though he has to be able to take some stiff blows in order to be able to keep on hitting.
—Admiral Ernest J. King

The first rule of winning: Don't beat yourself.
                    —Football adage

Losing gracefully doesn't mean losing graciously. So get tough. Pick one of the following game plans and run for daylight. No. 1— *We wuz robbed.* . . . You can claim that the ballot boxes were stuffed. You can certainly demand a recount. . . . No. 2—*My big mistake.* After Aaron Burr won the famous one-on-one, Alexander Hamilton's handlers maintained that their guy lost the duel because he refused to work on his outside shooting. A true fatal flaw. . . . No. 3—*I'll be back.* Fighter Mohammed Ali or Napoleon pioneered this one, but Ali's sound bites are better. . . . So suck up your gut, stay hungry and go down swinging.
                    —Robert Lipsyte

(*See* Perseverance, Resolution, Success.)

Workaholism

If you don't take a vacation, you're going to fall flat on your nose, and then I'm going to have to do your work.
                    —Ken Roman

If someone tells me, "I'm working 90 hours a week," I say, "You're doing something terribly wrong. I go skiing on the weekend. I go out with my buddies on Friday and party. *You've* got to do the same or you've got a bad deal. Put down a list of the things you're doing that make you work 90 hours, and ten of them have to be nonsense, or else somebody else has got to do them for you."
                    —Jack Welch

(*See* Dedication, Executive Health, Hard Work, Recreation.)

Writing

1. Never use a metaphor, simile, or other figure of speech which you are used to seeing in print.
2. Never use a long word when a short one will do.
3. If it is possible to cut a word out, always cut it out.
4. Never use the passive when you can use the active.
5. Never use a foreign phrase, a scientific word, or a jargon word if you can think of an everyday English equivalent.
6. Break any of these rules sooner than say anything outright barbarous.

                    —George Orwell

On writing business letters:
The first thing necessary in writing letters of business, is extreme clearness and perspicuity; every paragraph should be so clear, and unambiguous, that the dullest fellow in the world may not be able to mistake it, nor obliged to read it twice in order to understand it.

                    —Lord Chesterfield

                    (*See* Clarity.)

Y

Yes-Men

If you're really good at picking people, you use your power through them without stifling them. I work very hard at not recruiting yes-men, and that's hard to do in a big company, because if you knock them over the head two or three times, they will *become* yes-men. I tell them all the time, "I don't want you to become yes-men!"
                                —W. Michael Blumenthal

(*See* Sycophants.)

Z

Zero-Sum Game

Scheme not to make what's Another's your own;
Be not a Dog for the sake of a Bone.
            —Arthur Guiterman

(*See* Teamwork.)

Index